CHANGING *TO WIN*

CHANGING *TO WIN*

GILES LONG

PIATKUS

PIATKUS

First published in Great Britain in 2008 by Piatkus Books

A CIP catalogue record for this book
is available from the British Library

ISBN 978-0-7499-0992-5

Edited by Andrew John
Text design by Golddust Design
Illustrations by Rodney Paull
Typeset in Bembo by Palimpsest Book Production Ltd.,
Grangemouth, Stirlingshire
Printed and bound in Great Britain by Clays Ltd, St Ives plc

This is a work of non-fiction. However, the names and
identities of some of the people have been disguised to respect
and protect their privacy.

Piatkus Books
An imprint of
Little, Brown Book Group
100 Victoria Embankment
London EC4Y 0DY

An Hachette Livre UK Company
www.hachettelivre.co.uk

www.piatkus.co.uk

For my Mother, Father and Brother, who stood with
me staring into the darkest hours and who were
always there to celebrate the most glorious
of moments.

Contents

Acknowledgements

Joey Gardiner and Beverley Turner for their help in the early stages of writing, my brilliant editor Karen Farrington and Albert DePetrillo for his belief.

My coaches Mike Gosling, Ann Peterson, Janet Watkins, Graham Wilmott, Colin Hood and Rhys Gormley, and all the great training partners I've been privileged to swim with.

And my thanks to everyone else that helped me achieve my dreams – you know who you are.

Chapter One

The Secret of Success

With a pounding pulse in my ears, I carved out a well-worn rhythm in the waveless chlorine waters of Sydney's Olympic pool. The start had been only seconds before but now it seemed like a lifetime away as the wall came forward to meet my reaching hands.

Below the water everything appeared lagoon-blue and calm. The glimpses I saw above the pool were, by contrast, like a film on fast-forward, sepia through the smoked goggles sucked tightly into my eyes.

Little more than a minute after leaving the starting block, I was back in its shadow, swivelling my eyes to the scoreboard. My fist punched the humid air as I saw my name in lights – in first place and a record breaker. It was my moment of glory. Yet how did I achieve it?

There was nothing straightforward about the journey to Sydney, nothing was gifted to me, little had come easily. Natural swimming talent aside, it was a case of graft and grit, self-discipline and self-knowledge with a generous dose of durability to overcome the doubts.

I had harboured dreams of Olympic success since childhood. I have never thought of myself as a writer of books. Syntax, sentence construction and artful word play have not been high on my agenda, nor featured among the secret dreams that we all lock deep in our souls. But now I am labouring line by line over a laptop. This book will be a different achievement, in its way exciting, challenging and daunting, like my Olympic ambition.

And, if I was to write a book, anyone who knows me well would think its topic would indeed be swimming. After all, it's in this sport that I've won medals, broken records and achieved highest sporting ambition.

If not swimming, then the effects of cancer in childhood is another possible area of expertise. I had a bone tumour diagnosed when I was thirteen that recurred two years after I seemed to be cured.

In fact, the book that is opening up before you will be best placed on the business shelves. It is a tool to motivate yourself, as an individual, as part of a team and as a leader of a team. Based upon a simple idea, it will enable you to aspire to and achieve those huge goals in life, the real earth shakers.

At the same time, it's collapsible, so that you can use it to start writing that report (or that book). It is based on the foundation that *motivation* is sustained by *inspiration* and that the best fuel for that is *change*. Taking the starting syllables of those all important three words (though not in that order), I call it the *Chimo Cycle* ('chee-mo'). I'm a proud advocate of it because it works. My international swimming career is evidence of that.

Within days you'll be able to use the Chimo Cycle standing on your head, perhaps having customised it in your own mind. Since there is only one basic model, illustrated on these pages through a story, you are far more likely to remember it after you put the book down. Simple methods like this that can be remembered long after they have been imparted are the most powerful of all.

No one is more surprised than I to have fashioned a model that can change fortunes in the commercial world. It came about from drawing on those personal experiences that I've briefly mentioned, which cover the entire scale, from ecstatic to downright awful. In short, my own rocky road to success meant that motivation and inspiration wasn't always around. I had to learn to generate it and I had to change if I was going to win.

The Chimo Cycle wasn't something that I came up with while I was swimming. But when I analyse my career it's clear that I used Chimo Cycles throughout. It was the process that I went though to be my very best. Conversely, when I didn't use it, I was at my most mediocre.

Chimo uncovered

When I finished swimming I had a story to tell, one that I knew had resonance with the business community. My story was all about adaptation and aspiration, two vital components in commercial success, and I became a public speaker.

To assist in my new career I got a mentor, David Pearson, the former chief executive officer of Sony in Europe. The concept of mentoring is the provision of one-to-one personal support and encouragement, from a more accomplished business person to one with less experience.

During our discussions he explained to me the concept of a business tool called BOMMB, the acronym for base, objective, method, measurement and base.

In simple terms, you decide where you are, where you want to be, how you are going to get there and when you have got there, and then outline your new base. It's a well-worn method that springs easily to mind.

I loved the idea of coining forward momentum in such a way but I found this particular recipe to be unduly rigid. Personally, I wanted a process that was equally snappy but considerably more flexible. I examined my swimming career, littered with lows and highs, and eventually came up with three vital factors: change, inspiration and motivation.

And I quickly realised that, as a tight unit, they worked

beyond the confines of swimming and in just about every arena of life I could imagine. Indeed, I applied them to my new career of public speaking and the results were astonishing. An embryonic job swiftly turned into a full-blown busy occupation. I knew that Chimo would be with me for the rest of my life. More than that, I knew it would work for others, give them the drive necessary to achieve growth and goals in any arena.

But what is change? It's a word that people use all the time without ever stopping to say what they mean by it. Here's the *Oxford Concise English Dictionary* (10th Edition, 1999) definition: 'Change (verb): To make or become different, (noun) The action of changing; an instance of becoming different.'

Change is special because it is both a process and an outcome. Whether considered a change for better or for worse, it's very difficult to experience it without having at least a glimmer of an idea. An idea is often inspiring. If you can act on this idea you are by definition motivated and will do something. It's difficult to achieve anything without changing something. With change you have moved closer to the outcome of your goal – either directly or indirectly – while simultaneously starting the process all over again.

So, clearly, you're not going to get there unless you have some inspiration. Here's the definition of that: 'Inspiration (noun): The process or quality of being inspired; a sudden brilliant or timely idea.'

This is a process, but an elusive one. In interviews,

people are often asked, 'What or who was your in-spiration?' Often, the interviewee then rattles off a list of names, places or people. But what *was* it about those names, places or people that triggered their brilliant or timely idea? It's a mysterious quality but an essential one.

In the wake of inspiration comes motivation, defined like this: 'Motivation (noun): 1. A motive [for doing something], 2. Enthusiasm.' Usually it's presented as a process, one that drives you forth. How can that be? Surely it must be an outcome. You arrive at a point at which you have a motive or enthusiasm.

This model is: *Ch*ange > *I*nspiration > *Mo*tivation > Change – or the Chimo Cycle.

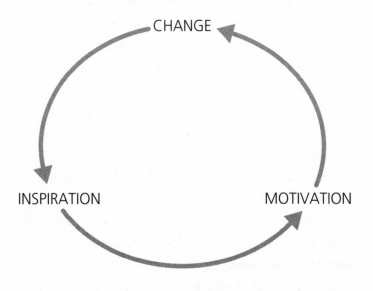

Figure 1. Basic Chimo Cycle diagram

It doesn't matter whether you start from the point of trying to achieve your lifetime goal or just wanting to finish the sentence you're writing, or you are searching for a larger goal. You just approach the model differently.

Daring to dream

If your dream is something huge, you may well consider it so outlandish that you haven't even told anyone about it. It's so far from where you currently consider yourself to be that you can't begin to comprehend what change you could possibly make to ignite the level of inspiration needed for the monumental amount of motivation you'll need to climb the mountain. In this instance, it's not the dream that is the problem. It's probably that you are attaching too small a time period to achieving it. For these kinds of dream, it can take years (it took me thirteen) – a prospect in itself that is a classic motivation killer.

However, if you have one of these dreams, I expect you can identify the area in which you might make the first step. After taking that step, you'll have a far better idea of what lies ahead. In essence you are building a series of small Chimo Cycles that will be able to support a larger, slower-turning one. After you've linked together a few of these larger ones, you can use those to support something even bigger.

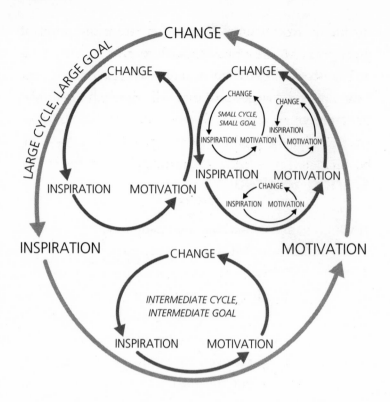

The smaller the chimo cycle, the more robust it is. Keep making them smaller until you find a personal 'foundation' cycle of inspiring change.

Figure 2. Fitting small Chimo Cycles into a larger one:
'Base cycles'

It's not only about a mighty dream. Perhaps you're at a low ebb for one reason or another. The big one is not even on the agenda at the moment and you just want to get going again in some small way. Perhaps, in your busy life, you know what you want but there never seems to be any time to achieve it. This is when the smallest of Chimo Cycles gets drawn on a blank piece of paper. The problem is how to start it.

That start will come from one of two places. Someone will say or do something that will alter your perceptions and spark an idea. Or you can make the change yourself. The former, as parts of this book show, can be incredibly powerful. Unfortunately, you might be

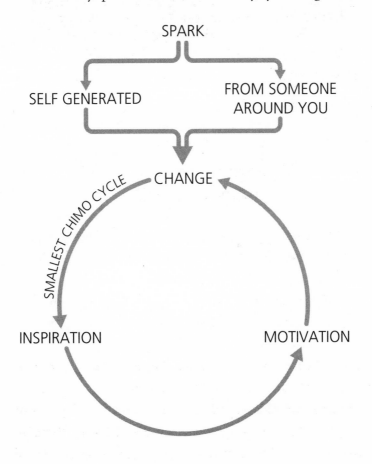

Figure 3. Initial 'spark' diagram

waiting a long time for that pivotal moment. The latter is much more demanding – even if that necessary nugget is inside you the whole time. It is at your disposal whenever you choose to use it.

The pinnacle of achievement in the sport of swimming is to win a gold medal at the Olympic or Paralympic Games. There is just one week of competition every four years at which an entire team have to be at the absolute zenith of their performing abilities. The only problem is that there are short events and long ones, all swum across four different strokes.

The training regime required for an athlete to be at their best for the 50-metres freestyle is completely different from that needed for the 200-metre breaststroke, which in turn is different from the 1,500-metre freestyle. All three competitors will need to hit form at the games and will be expected to do so collectively at other large competitions along the way, though at a range of smaller competitions underneath that layer they will be not always be at their peak: the sprinter will be close to their best every time; the 200-metre swimmer three or four times a year; with the 1,500-metre swimmer possibly hitting a best time only once each season.

Team performance

There are many models for improving performance across a team in a commercial environment, but most seem to have an inherent inefficiency built into them. They require the entire team to move through a series of steps at exactly the same time, no matter what they are trying to achieve. You decide where you are, then where you would like to be and how you are going to get there; before looking back to see if you made it and anchoring your new ground to start the process all over again.

This is fantastic if you have a team of people who are able to all operate within a rigid structure guaranteed to move forward without interruption, delay or setback to any one individual. Few are lucky enough to work like that. Most inevitably end up getting the most from the majority of people while a few on the periphery are left to try to fit in the best they can. The team functions, often very well, but not at its true potential, because there are a few within the team who are never quite able to draw on the power of change as a motivational tool; they are washed along by it.

It's not for me to tell you how to organise your team – and, yes, you do lead a team of at least one. You need to decide the objective, but then create a framework so that each individual can rotate through their own individual Chimo Cycle. Once again, it can be focused at a fairly low target level to ensure that people keep fairly close to hitting regular deadlines together, or at a much higher level where people are at completely different stages for a long time, coming together only for a big launch event.

If you can get each member of your team to look for change that will give them a spark of inspiration and you are able to give them flexibility, choose the level of Chimo Cycle they engage in as their base layer, then you will have a happy and motivated team. However, nobody will have any interest in being more motivated if you aren't yourself.

Many people's professional and recreational lives are kept completely separate – and for good reason. But the motivating power of change lies across both. Perhaps in your professional life you used to say, 'I want to be in position x by age y.' As time passed by you've got into a comfortable routine whereby you answer your emails at the same time each day, you follow the same structure in all your presentations and have the same lunch. In your recreational life you've always wanted to run a marathon, taken the first step by starting running, but always taken the same route. Or wanted to be able to paint well, or play an instrument but always ended up starting with the same subject matter or the same tune.

Imagine

Just imagine if you changed something right now. If instead of painting that bowl of fruit you went to the nearest service station to capture the mood of some of the customers. The end result may well end up being something you wouldn't even hang in the downstairs toilet. But that change will give you something far more valuable. An idea. Perhaps you'll end up going back to the service station after all with a way to compose the picture better. I bet those two pictures get painted in quick succession, after you have left the brushes idle for weeks. With one seemingly small change you have moved closer to becoming the painter you've always wanted to be in your last two paintings than you did with the previous dozen.

The same happens with the instrument or the marathon. Perhaps you play the same tune or run the same route but do it faster or more slowly. On tomorrow's run you're going to see if you can keep your heart rate the same for the entire circuit, regardless of the uphill and downhill sections. After a few tries you manage it, so how long before you can do it in a faster time?

At work you maybe had a dream job in mind and were considered a critical part of the team. These days you feel a bit adrift. Your team seems to move forward like an advancing fleet and, although you're right in the pack, you can't quite remember the last time you had unbroken water in front of you. Maybe the reason that you're not making progress as you used to is that the weather's changed but you've set your sail the same way you always have.

Then again, you may be the complete opposite. You know exactly where you want to be and you've tried changing everything but just don't seem to make progress. The dream job hangs there almost as if it had deliberately been positioned to torment you. It feels as if you're doing everything right but it's just outside your control, and, although you are still motivated, you know it's not going to be long before your enthusiasm chokes. Is it time to write that dream job on a piece of paper and stick it to the wall? Free your mind from it, just for a bit. It may be time to look at revisiting some of those changes you've already made, only this time use them to draw more fundamental ideas rather than hope it will be the silver-bullet solution. After all, no club-level athlete went straight to Olympic level from just one elementary technical change, but many have done so after making a whole series.

I didn't need a Chimo Cycle to start swimming, though. Water is my element. I love it. It fascinates, mesmerises and captivates me. I could stare at it for hours. Fickle by nature, it'll make you believe in its eternal abundance but take any opportunity just to trickle way. I've felt like that since I can ever remember, hypnotised by this miracle of creation.

When I was young I can remember how other children would always wish to be a bird and fly. I could never understand why. When you are underwater you *are* flying. So, if you can already fly, what is the point in burning up your wish on something you can already do? It was this love of being in the water that my parents spotted and why they encouraged me to join the local swimming club when I was seven. It was the first step into a new world.

Perhaps you are already thinking, 'I'm not sure I felt that way about anything when I was that age. Is this story going to have any relevance to me?' However, just because I liked being in the water and swimming fast, it does not mean that I liked the early-morning starts for training. Or the seemingly endless number of swimming competitions at draughty pools that burned up an entire weekend and often ended without any improvement at all. They were some of the stepping stones that I had to touch in order to reach my dream.

The journey has taken me to some frighteningly dark lows and some dazzling highs. I had to learn how to motivate myself and others; to give inspiration as well as keep pathways in my mind open so inspiration could find me. On the days when it didn't, I had to work out how I was going to dredge some up.

I was part of the Great Britain swimming team for almost fourteen years and went to three Paralympic Games, winning gold medals at two of them, breaking the world record at one. In that time I also went to four World Championships, three European Championships and countless other national and international competitions. I held the world record in the 100-metre butterfly for almost ten years.

I have been part of club, national and international teams. Some of those have been highly motivated medal-generating machines and some have let stagnation become the lethal injection to progress. I have seen motivation evaporate in a successful team in front of an audience of thousands because of poor direction, and seen it built from nothing on a cold outdoor poolside with not a competition in sight.

Above all, I have learned there are the times when you feel as if you were flying and nothing seems impossible. There isn't a piece of paper in the world large enough for you to be able to draw the Chimo Cycle you're chomping your way through. But it isn't always like that. There are also days when every last molecule of water is putting up a fight, and pushing yourself for just a few more seconds seems insurmountable.

When we are first at school we are taught through stories. Yet, as we get older, that powerful form of teaching seems to disappear. People have been using stories to pass on ideas since the dawn of time – from paintings on cave walls, to hieroglyphics in ancient Egyptian temples, to the discovery of gravity by Sir Isaac Newton, when an apple, we are told, fell on his head. Tales and fables are an unparalleled way of passing on information and ideas, while at the same time providing colour, context and example to give them the best possible chance of being remembered and used.

The following chapters are my story.

Chapter Two

About a Boy

In my very early years I was primarily concerned with locating, acquiring and consuming sweets. That and trying to ascertain among friends who was better – Batman or Spiderman. I would spend whatever time was left of my time tearing about the White Court housing estate in Braintree, Essex, on my prized BMX bike.

We moved there in 1979, when my younger brother turned up and demanded more space. It was newly built on the site of an old Second World War American army hospital. The hospital had long since gone but its water tower still stood, solitary in a field of long grass. The flat fields were initially bisected by roads that had been laid but awaited houses. Before long each space was filled.

Riverside, Braintree's swimming pool, had opened in 1976, the year I was born. As a family we would go regularly. My parents were sailors and it was seen as an important survival skill. Sailing had taken my parents to all sorts of interesting places – to Australia in the early seventies when long-haul flying was rare and the 'jet set' was a phrase that really meant something. They had also sailed on a lake in Poland, journeying behind the Iron Curtain and driving through East Germany.

My parents are both incredible people who have sets of skills that complement each other. Mum is a determined and driven woman. She grew up on a farm in the middle of nowhere in rural Essex. My granddad worked the land and didn't see the value in education for women. At sixteen she was presented with the option of having her bedroom redecorated or going to college. It still makes me chuckle a little that he thought that was a balanced choice. Already she knew that the only way out of rural isolation was a set of good exam grades, so the bedroom would have to wait. After that, she went to work for the stockbrokers Campbell Johnston Associates as a secretary in the City. Within four years she was on the board.

Education was an entirely different experience for Dad, who grew up in east London. His secondary school was a war zone, with pupils and teachers often involved in fights and a French teacher who had been driven partially insane in a Japanese prisoner-of-war camp. Fortunately, Dad is a gifted artist and went on to become a technical illustrator. He understands materials like no one else I've seen. His love of making things has meant that there really hasn't been a time when something wasn't under construction in the house or shed: clay sculptures, model aeroplanes, lights for the house, or furniture. When I was very young it was always boats. My parents were part of a small group of people who first brought the 18-foot skiff to the UK. Designed in Australia, it's a dinghy that carries as much sail as an 18-foot boat will handle, and makes other sail-driven craft look as if they were travelling through glue.

Sport has always been a feature of family life, although I can never remember watching sport on TV when I was very young. The first time I was really aware of football was the 1986 World Cup in Mexico, and even then it was puzzling that all my friends wanted to spend their money on stickers, which came a poor second to sweets in my view. But in 1983 when I was seven I was sitting in the back of the car as Mum drove us up to the swimming pool. She glanced into the rear-view mirror and said, 'Would you like to join the swimming club?'

I didn't start doing back flips at the idea, I was shy and, underneath it all, I still am. I found the idea daunting. Meeting other kids from strange schools, well, I wasn't sure about that. But I enjoyed swimming enough to give it a go. I passed the necessary entry test and began going three times a week, rising quickly to four times a week, before it was upped to five. I ended up training in a lane with a load of girls. Yuk! To make matters worse, they were all better than I was. My friends were training in the lane above and seemed to be having a fantastic time. But, every time I put my head in the water and started moving, it was magic. I loved the feel of the water, the way it eddied and the way it could be sculpted.

Olympic dreams

During Christmas 1983, just three months after I joined the swimming club, I was given the Kingfisher *Children's Factfinder*. It was a huge blue book with lots of small pictures on the front and contained within it were the secrets of the entire world. On Page 177 there was a small paragraph in the margin that merely said, 'At the 1972 Olympic Games in Munich Mark Spitz won seven gold medals and set seven world records in the sport of swimming.' Together with a badly drawn cartoon, twenty-three words inspired me to go to the Olympics and win a gold medal.

However, my ambitions had an early setback. My first swimming competition was the club championships in November 1984. All the races were over short distances, typically just one length of the 25-metre pool. I didn't get a single medal and it was tough being beaten by my friends. There was virtually no competitive sport at school, so it was all a bit of a shock. I was disappointed to leave with a small set of ribbons, awarded to those in the minor places. When I got home I showed them to my mum with an indolent wave of my hand, but she made an effort to look at them and put them on display in the lounge. I thought this was a bit odd because some of the other boys' parents hadn't been that interested, even though they had won a medal. One of my friends had been interrogated by his dad as to why he hadn't swum faster – even though he'd won.

I'd also encountered Ian Mackenzie for the first time, an incredible breaststroke swimmer. Breaststroke was by far my worst stroke and I hated it; but when he swam it was like watching an effortless dance. There were no stops, breaks or still points in the stroke cycle, just forward motion with the leg-kick and the hand-pull in near-perfect synchronisation. He was four years older than I, and everyone was sure that he would reach the absolute apex of sporting achievement. If I needed any motivation, well, he was it.

And, when my parents asked me if I'd enjoyed the competition, I had to admit that, in a way, I had. I hadn't enjoyed picking up a series of ribbons. In truth, I'd hated it and preferred being disqualified, walking away with nothing. But I had established a whole set of personal best times that were mine and no one could touch. Next time, I could go back and win – against my times and my friends. This was not an instantaneous enjoyment that you got from eating sweets or playing. That was light-bulb enjoyment: when it was switched on it shined brightly, but as soon as it was off it was over instantly. This pleasure had a series of components: thrilling, frightening, disappointing, tiring. But it was almost as fun looking back at doing it as it was actually doing it.

I had never felt as if I were doing something that most people didn't until I was round at Kevin Howlett's house. His family were from Liverpool and the 1986 FA Cup final was between Liverpool and arch-rivals Everton. It seemed as if there were hundreds of us all watching the television and it was the first time that I had ever watched a match from start to finish. It seemed a stressful affair. The mood plummeted after a second-rate first-half performance by the Reds. I didn't dare move throughout the whole of half-time. After a resurgent Liverpool ended up scoring three times in the second half, winning the match 3–1, there was jubilation. I didn't understand how they could feel that way about the success of a group of people they didn't even know.

After a while attention shifted to me. Someone asked me what sports I liked and we talked about swimming for a bit. But, when I said that I went swimming at 8 a.m. on Sundays, they all gasped in disbelief. This was the first time I was aware of the important difference between watching and doing.

By the age of nine I started to emerge as a back-stroker and began to beat people of my age, although over only short distances. Then in the summer of 1986 came the real crunch. I moved out of the junior club and into the intermediate squad, which meant the start of weekday early-morning training. No longer were evening training sessions enough. I announced to my parents that they were going to have to get up at 5.15 a.m. to get me to the pool for a 6 a.m. start. Mum flatly refused but Dad was a little more measured. As long as I set my alarm and got up and then went to wake one of them up we would go. All of a sudden it became a challenge.

The night before, I could hardly get to sleep. The thought of getting up when no one else was about made it feel like going on holiday. My alarm clock was of the type whose numbers flick over on little plastic flaps, like a miniature Rolodex. With its curved white plastic case and hi-tech-like black number configuration at the front, it looked like something out of *Star Wars*.

When it buzzed I flicked it off and jumped out of bed – I'd woken just in time to see the minutes flick over.

That summer Ian Mackenzie had become European junior champion at just fourteen. He raced boys two years older than he was from all over Europe and he had beaten them all. I was so fired up. I went into my parents' room to wake up Dad. Ten minutes later we were in the car; ten minutes after that at the pool.

I got changed and made my way down to the pool-side. I felt tiny. At early-morning sessions the pool was split between my group, of which I was one of the youngest, and the top squad. It was my first taste of an elite team.

Some kids got out early to get to school but I stayed in right until the end of the session at 7.30. That day in September 1986 I had so much confidence. I didn't have to be shy Giles any more.

That night I felt absolutely shattered, but Dad and I

agreed to go again the following day. I went to bed early and the next morning was a bit harder. The following morning I didn't make it. I was so fast asleep that even with the alarm clock next to my head I kept on sleeping. But the rhythm of the week was largely established.

Drowning, not waving

The final year of primary school was one of the happiest. My classmates were real characters. We had a lot of fun and I had a strong group of friends at the swimming club too. Underlying this great year, though, was fear. It was my last year at White Court Primary before I went to Chelmer Valley High. White Court School was just around the corner; Chelmer Valley was thirty minutes' drive away.

In the July of 1987 I turned eleven. The summer holidays began and I swam at the County Championships and Southern Counties Regional Championships. Nationals were next on the list. But the swimming club closed down for most of August and I began to stew. My friends seemed to be going different ways.

With trepidation, I arrived at senior school and was assigned to my form. Kevin Howlett was in the same class. We registered in a form room where Mrs Rowland, a formidable home-economics teacher, told us our timetable. We were also put into houses. Whatever *they* were. Mine was called Jackman, whoever *he* was, and the others were Eden, Stephens and Palmer.

I would love to be able to write that I took it all in my stride and that I saw every new challenge as an opportunity, but in truth I was buckling. Shy Giles was back and there seemed no amount of swimming in the world that could send him away again. There was change everywhere but this wasn't the Chimo Cycle in action. This was fear. It too is a great motivator but only for short infrequent periods of time.

Swimming training was getting harder with more sessions expected each week. Secondary school meant homework and with the added travel time there just didn't seem enough time in my day. School finished at 3.25 p.m. The bus stop was about a seven-minute walk away and the bus company had conveniently timed it so that the bus arrived at 3.30 p.m. and then again at 4 p.m. If I ran for the 3.30 p.m. bus, it meant that I got home with enough time to have something to eat before going training. If I got the bus half an hour later I still had enough time to do everything I needed to. So why did I get so wound up about getting the earlier one? I have no idea.

Music hath charms

The only thing I ever wanted to do other than win gold at the Olympics was to be a rock star. So I decided to learn the violin. Anyone who wanted to learn an instrument could have music lessons at school in place of another lesson, so long as they kept up with schoolwork.

Three off us had a violin lesson at the same time with Mr Rhys. Rebecca, whose violin looked as if someone had cleaned it with a Brillo pad, was learning because her mum wanted her to; Andrew was learning because he always had; and I was learning because I wanted to be on *Top of the Pops*. Upon reflection, I see it was an odd choice.

Looking back, I see that life was easy enough, but at the time the stress was burying me. School, homework, violin, travel, swimming – everything in my life seemed to be conspiring to put me back into the buttoned-down box of shyness and uncertainty. It was a box I'd always lived in but one that I could leave for short periods at will. But it was starting to feel as if the lid was being slowly closed for ever. Schoolkids are like pike: they pick off the weakest. That's when the bullying started.

Dual life

It always starts with 'little' things. The flick of a door from the person in front, a foot stuck out in the corridor or the hiding of my violin (though perhaps I should have been grateful for that). I had always been a boy at school who cried a lot and that must have hung there like a prize. 'See if you can make Giles cry.' The swimming club was becoming my only release. Lots of people came together, pursuing a common goal and enjoying themselves despite tough mornings and hard training sessions. It felt as if I were living a dual life.

Unfortunately, Chimo is not a panacea for the problem of bullying. Everyone loathes a bully and bullying is wrong, but that is not much comfort when it's happening to you.

One night, after a schoolyard skirmish, I got home and felt awful, as if something was going to break inside me. I wondered if there was anyone else out there like me. School felt as if it stifled all creativity. It was learning by numbers and no one shone.

Ian Mackenzie had fallen out with the head coach, Tony MacGuinness, about a year previously, at a great cost to British sport. He was one of the most prodigiously talented swimmers I've ever been in a pool with. On top of everything I had an intermittently sore shoulder, which was starting to impact on my swimming. I was desperate for something to change.

Well, be careful what you wish for because you might just get it.

Chapter Three

As Bad as it Gets

University College Hospital (UCH) is buried right in the heart of England's capital. This caused some friction between driver Dad and navigator Mum. Mum knew exactly where to go just after we had staked a claim in the wrong lane or taken a wrong turn. Dad would emit words of friction, impairing Mum's concentration sufficiently for us to miss the next turn. After circling various blocks viciously we arrived and parked just off Gower Street. Dad poured the Mexican national debt into the parking meter and my heart sank more with every coin's clatter. The journey had been superseded by the destination.

The hospital stood before me like some giant redbrick fortress. It was raining, just enough to turn the dirt of the pavement into bitumen-black wallpaper paste. With my parents at either side I walked into the huge building to be confronted by a foyer that was a flagship of late-eighties NHS underfunding. We set about locating the reception desk.

My parents had all the necessary information and said that we were going to 'Private Patients Ward Two'. At the time we had no idea that hospital orientation required a degree in navigation and the stamina of a camel. When we eventually found the reception desk it became perfectly obvious why it had been so expertly concealed. The woman on the desk had about as much knowledge of the location of PPW2 as the specific whereabouts of the capital of Burkina Faso. After phoning the entire hospital and asking almost every available passer-by, she said, 'Why not try the fifth floor? The lift's just around the corner and on your right.'

We stepped into the lift and pressed 5. It must have been a popular choice, as it was the only broken button. We announced ourselves to the sister and said that we had an appointment to see Dr Jonathon Shamash. She was with us right until the moment when we said whom we'd come to see. Subsequently, we headed down to the third floor. Upon arriving at the *second* floor, after a brief but enthralling visit to the fourth, we had found PPW2.

Lunchtime had only just ended and the smell of stale food prevailed. Everyone in PPW2 was connected to or in the process of becoming acquainted with an intravenous drip. It seemed to me that the vast majority of people in this ward were probably more than just a little off colour. As Dad wandered off to find Dr Shamash

I contemplated the name of the ward 'Private Patients Ward Two'. This was not a private ward in any sense. My parents were not paying for treatment, nor were patients being treated behind closed doors.

This contemplation was, however, short-lived as a youngish, short man with unkempt black hair and the posture of a semi-deflated bouncy castle sidled over and ushered the three of us into a large bedded room. He showed us to one of the beds, and Mum sat on the chair next to it, with Dad, the doctor and me sitting on it. I sat near the top of the bed resting my back on the pillows; I rearranged them and looked up, and noticed that the others were all looking at me. It seemed the only way this was going to get more ominous was if it started raining again. I glanced to my left and out of the window. It did.

Finally, the doctor spoke. 'After the tests we've done, the, er, X-rays, blood tests and the biopsy' – he glanced at a chart – 'we've diagnosed you as having an osteosarcoma of the right humerus.' I looked at Mum, then Dad and back at the doctor. Why did they all keep looking at me? Not even the briefest of glances at one another. And what on earth was an osteo-thingy in my right humorous? Funny? If so *I* was still awaiting the punchline. There was a brief silence in which the doctor sensed my failure to grasp the situation. 'It is a bone tumour,' he added. 'It's a form of cancer.'

I could feel my innards imploding, my time slowing, a screeching of tyres as my life ground to a halt.

As quickly as these feelings came they ebbed away. All of a sudden they were just a collection of redundant thoughts. I was ready for the conversation to commence again. What kind of expression I had had on my face, and for how long, I didn't know. It just felt blank.

'I want to use a course of chemotherapy' – more jargon, I thought – 'to shrink the tumour as much as possible before we operate.' OK, so there were slightly more words that I recognised, but it was still very much happening to someone else. 'There are side effects to this form of treatment: for one your hair will fall out and you'll feel sick and suffer from nausea and vomiting.'

'When do you want to start?' Dad spoke for the first time since we all sat on the bed.

'Today, now if possible.' The doctor motioned as he spoke, and my parents both nodded with melancholy resignation. Once again, all eyes fixed on me. I could feel dread setting in. Panic. My mind was racing. I could feel the excuse department of my brain going into overdrive. The end result of my mental exertions was unimpressive. I blurted out, 'But I haven't got any stuff, you know, toothbrush and stuff. I need my stuff.' All I wanted to do was get out and go home. Go anywhere.

'It's OK,' said Dad. 'Mum, or I can bring you an overnight bag.' Dad, do you want to just shut up? I thought. You're really *not* helping the situation, I didn't say. The doctor went away to ask the sister about admitting me to the ward.

'Mum, I don't want to stay here tonight,' I whispered

in a harsh tone, hoping that, by my appealing to her, proceedings could somehow be changed to my liking.

'It'll be all right, darling.' Great! First of all Dad had me walking the plank; then my own mother holds the cutlass to my back. I was out of ideas.

The doctor rounded the doorframe and entered the room again, disappointment on his face. 'I'm afraid that there aren't any beds available at the moment, so we'll have to start later in the week.' I could have jumped the 40 miles home, I was so relieved. It did cross my mind that if there weren't any beds available then what had we all been sitting on? This was an idea that didn't need to be aired. Who was *I* to argue with the good doctor?

The three of us gathered up our things and set about saying goodbye and thank you. We turned right out of the room and back towards the stairs, passing the sister in the corridor, who said that she had our phone number and would call to arrange the best time to come in.

Making my way down the stairs I thought, 'Now, now indeed. He must be mad. Hospitals aren't supposed to work like that. Nothing happens *now*.' You phone someone up (whom you never speak to again), they tell you to be at a room on a certain day and time, you go to the room, wait a couple of hours, see someone who tells you to see someone else, you do a bit of phoning around for no particular reason and then when the problem has finally become sufficiently acute you see someone else and something is done. That's how it worked, of this I was sure.

More than a big break

Events leading up to that hospital visit had been far from glorious. Ironically, the playground bullies who had put me there ended up as heroes to some. Life at that point really was not brilliant.

It was thanks to an injury I sustained from them that doctors discovered for the first time that I was suffering from cancer. But let's be clear: when my arm was broken by some Neanderthal idiots one lunchtime my long-term health and swimming career was the last thing on the perpetrators' minds.

On 15 September 1989 I had just started my third year. The previous July I had turned thirteen. Life was unremarkable apart from the ongoing problem of a pulled muscle in my right shoulder, attributed to intense swimming training. I had had some ultrasound and heat treatment after initially seeing my GP. The treatments seemed to work for short periods before the problem returned.

At school I was standing on the school field with my friends talking about the important matters of teenage politics. As we flexed unlikely truths with one another, I noticed, some distance away, two boys from my year. David Bartley and Simon Foster were selecting a series of victims in short order. Holding a leg of a victim aloft and kicking the other away was their chosen activity. The result was one collapsed child in no small amount of pain.

Suddenly, out of the blue, the leg kickers loomed. My group scattered haphazardly into a larger radius, all the time laughing nervously. No one wanted to appear weak. I tried to distance myself in a sort of casual retreat. As my smile muscles started to tire, Bartley and Foster headed my way. Running away was not an option, as Bartley held the school record for the 400 metres. I knew I would shortly have a close look at the grass.

A small crowd had gathered waiting to witness another Bartley slaying. He got to a range of 3 metres and his size grew exponentially with every passing moment. Within the briefest space of time he had become ten storeys high and I surrendered to the inevitable. He grabbed my left leg, raised it to ninety degrees. I looked the mindless thug in the eyes and saw the simple brain that powered the actions and the smile. Why did I feel so inferior?

Thwack! His leg swept my right foot clean away. My head and body began a long journey to the floor, where so many others had been before. The ground was hard, baked by previous hot days. As I hit the ground it felt as if I had been run down by an express train. Laughter of those around me was shrill in my ears. But no one laughed so raucously as Bartley and his henchman Foster. At least the deed was done. I could get up now and stand by and watch someone else become one of Bartley's statistics.

I had fallen on my right side but had flopped onto my front. Pressing both hands on the ground, I attempted to get up. From the top of my right arm, around where my pulled shoulder muscle had been, came a peculiar grinding sensation. As I tried to put weight on it, a sharp excruciating pain shot though my body. I collapsed back on my front and burst into tears, as much with shock as with pain. The immediate reaction from those around remained the same. Expectedly so, since I had been no stranger to shedding a few tears in my school career.

A dinner lady was soon on the scene and got me to my feet. Only then did I look around at all those who had watched. There weren't the laughing faces I had expected. Some were confused, some kids walking away, most concerned. Bartley was already being escorted to the head's office. Clutching my arm I walked with the dinner lady towards the first aid room.

It was on the ground floor, next to the office of head, Mrs Marsham. Manoeuvring delicately down the narrow corridor, I had to pass Bartley. Mrs Marsham was a formidable woman who, in this untested of incidents, could be capable of anything. As I passed Bartley he looked up at me and clearly thought this too. Good.

The school nurse, Mrs Gillam, asked my name in her precise Scottish accent while putting my arm in a sling. With a swift turn and an efficient hand she pulled my file from the cabinet in the corner of the room. Soon, she announced Dad was on his way as Mum was unavailable. I sat with my back against the wall watching nothing happen. The bell rang, signalling the end of the lunch break and the start of afternoon registration. The first of the afternoon lessons came and went. Twisting my arm slightly, I realised why I had avoided doing so.

Effortlessly Mrs Gillam entered the room with Mr Watson, the bearded deputy head, behind her. 'Mr Watson is going to drive you to casualty. Your father said he can't get here for a while.' Carefully, I got up, ostentatiously clutching my arm — I wanted to make it look as though I was in as much pain as possible. 'Thank you, Mrs Gillam.' Mr Watson felt around his suit pockets and produced a set of keys. The care I had taken getting up had prevented the shooting pain I had felt earlier, but not got rid of the pestle-and-mortar grinding sensation from deep inside my shoulder.

Interrogation

I was no stranger to the casualty (or A and E, as it's mostly called today) waiting room at the hospital.

We went to the reception desk, made the necessary declarations, took a seat and began working our way to the front of the list. 'So how did it happen?' Mr Watson asked after a brief pause. It had completely slipped my mind that the preceding events were still a mystery to him.

'A boy tripped me up,' I mumbled, looking towards the floor and hoping that would provide a satisfactory conclusion.

'Who?' came the sharp response.

'David Bartley,' I droned as if I'd said it a thousand times.

'Is he in your year?'

'Yes.'

'Well, how did he trip you up?'

'He held one of my legs and kicked the other away.'

Sometimes the worst form of interrogation you can have is when people are trying to help you. They're patient and understanding but force you to relive an ordeal that has not been to your gain. I was glad that all my battles for the day appeared over but sooner or later I was going to admit that I was bullied and, to me, that meant weakness, a character trait not part of the curriculum at Chelmer Valley High.

'He *grabbed*, your leg, while he *kicked* the other one away?' I nodded as I turned to look at him. It was the first time in the two years, at secondary school, that I noticed how bulky he was. And his heavily lined face with its thick moustache and beard was becoming weightier with every passing moment. I had to look away. 'What did he think he was doing?'

I shrugged. A short while turned into a long wait, which in turn highlighted the incredible level of discomfort delivered by the seats in the waiting room.

Dad appeared from the flank of my vision. He wore his pissed-off face, which promptly morphed itself into his concerned face, as he glanced towards my arm in its sling. 'In the wars again, mate?'

'Yeah.'

'Hello,' said Dad, turning to Mr Watson and holding out his hand. 'Bruce Long.'

'Mike Watson.'

The two engaged in a gripping handshake. Mr Watson then set about regaling the story. Dad remained standing and nodded gravely throughout, and then they shook hands again, we said goodbye and he left to go back to what little remained of the school day.

Dad sat down next to me on the plastic, bottle-green chair that had been previously occupied by Mr Watson. 'So who is this *boy*?'

The interrogation started again. It went along familiar lines until Dad waded in with an outraged, 'What did he *think* he was doing?'

'Having a laugh, I s'pose.'

'A *laugh*? Wait till I see his father!'

Throughout the whole of our conversation, Dad had not raised his voice once due to the ever-present signs requesting quiet. Instead his teeth had become progressively more clenched and his speech more aerated.

Our conversation continued sporadically as new ideas and unanswered questions popped into Dad's head. We were on the verge of running over the whole thing again when we were called through to see a doctor. He examined me, with hands the temperature of liquid nitrogen, feeling and prodding his way around my upper arm, asking if certain things hurt. Then, after I'd run over the whole story with him, we made our way to the X-ray department with orders that afterwards we go to the children's ward.

We waited in the X-ray department. Waited some more. Started to run over everything again. Then a radiographer called me into the X-ray room. 'If you'd just lie on the table . . .' She gestured towards the thin bed in the middle of the room. It was the end of a long day. Any delicate touch she had all but evaporated. Finally, having bent me into position, she walked over to the machine, which was over the other side of the room. I watched, amazed, as this enormous contraption glided across the room towards me, propelled solely by one person. With a few more clicks and adjustments a rectangle of light was targeted over my broken arm. A loud whirring lasted less than a second, engulfed the room, vanished and was replaced by a background hum. After just a few minutes we were told to make our way to the children's ward.

As I clasped my right arm at the elbow, we made

our way down the corridors. Eventually we pushed our way past an eight-foot bunny that had a door painted on its back and made our way to the nurses' station. They already knew who I was and with space-age efficiency I was led to a bed in a room of two. Dad and I sat on the bed and looked at each other. A doctor entered with the X-ray in his hand. 'Hi, Giles, I'm Doctor James and you must be Mr Long.'

'Hello,' said Dad brightly.

'Hi,' I mumbled.

His surname was actually Smith, James being his first name, but he seemed cool rather than embarrassing. 'You can see the break here,' he said as he jammed the X-ray under the clip of the light box on the wall. He had somehow managed to turn the light box on and just throw the X-ray into place all with one movement of the hand. 'It's a clean break right near the top of the bone here.' He pointed. It certainly was. A ball of bone was floating like a small moon inside my shoulder suspended over the pillar of light that it was previously joined to. 'The break is very high, so we're going to pin the top and bottom parts together. Unfortunately, the operating theatre is now closed so I'm afraid you'll have to wait until tomorrow for the operation. I'll go and see about getting you some painkillers.'

'Oh, OK.' Dad had either abandoned or got bored talking about David Bartley and his actions, and so we just sat and talked about other things.

Ward worries

Mum turned up with a bag of clothes and a thinly veneered fury that was going to be cooled only by her hearing the whole story herself at first hand. What she got was Dad telling it, second-hand, with me interjecting every time the facts started to become a bit loose.

I looked through the bag Mum had brought me. I wasn't going to be the most stylish person on the ward. Mum went home as it started to get dark to make sure that my brother was all right. I chatted with Dad until around ten thirty, and then he too had to go.

'See you tomorrow, sport. Keep smiling.'

His use of Aussie lingo always made me smile. Just as he was leaving, the nurse came into the room and gave me a small plastic cup with two white pills inside. 'Here are some painkillers. Oh, you haven't got any water. I'll fix that for you.' She bustled out of the room. Dad then kissed me on the head and went too.

With nothing else to do, I got ready for bed. I brushed my teeth with my left hand, putting as much toothpaste up my nose as in my mouth. I got undressed and squeezed in between the crisp white bed sheets, which had been so tightly tucked in that I thought a pair of scissors would have been useful. The nurse came back with some water. I swallowed the pills. 'If you need anything, just press the buzzer by your bed.' She lifted a handheld button, with a little illuminated nurse on it, and put it on the bed. Lying down like a corpse, I fell into a dreamless but disturbed sleep.

The corridor outside the room was filled with the clattering sounds of trolleys of all shapes and sizes being wheeled around, sorting out patients with their break-fasts, tablets and other necessities. I waited expectantly. The trolleys moved on and the noise outside the door dropped to its previous low level. Then I noticed a sign hung above my pillows that read 'Nil by mouth'. A bubbly nurse opened the door.

'Rise an'—Oh, you're up already.'

'Yeah, erm, how long before my operation?' I wasn't fazed by the prospect.

'It'll be early this afternoon.'

'Can I drink anything?' My mouth felt like sand and glue.

'A few small sips this morning, but nothing after that, all right? Give a buzz if you need anything.' She walked out of the room and I quickly gulped down a large cup of water and felt instantly guilty.

I sat on my bed. Walked over and looked out of the window. Saw the car park outside. Went to sit back on the bed. Got up again. Walked across the room. Messed about with the switches that operated the lights on the X-ray viewer on the wall. Knowing it wasn't a toy, I gingerly turned one of the four boxes on. With a *blung, bl-blung*, the top right box flickered and lit up. Momentarily I studied the way it emitted a uniform hard-white light across every part of its surface area. Then I turned it off. I turned it back on, and then off again.

Feeling more daring, I turned the top two on. By the time I'd turned all four on I got the fear and quickly got back onto my bed afraid a nurse would catch me. I sat there for no more than thirty seconds. Driven back to the light boxes on the opposite wall by boredom, I put a finger from my left hand on each of the switches. I turned the bottom two on, then the top two, bottom left and top right, top left and bottom right. Both right lights, both left lights, and then in changing timings and frequency.

I watched the brilliant white light give the day-lit room an artificial feel. But there was one last card to play. Aside from the four white switches that each controlled one box, there was a red switch. It was a good job it wasn't the self-destruct button, because, in the two seconds' thought I had given the matter, there was *no way* I was going to leave that switch alone. With three of the boxes on, I flicked it and they all went out. When it was flicked back to its original position, they all came back on. Oh, joy of joys! This was a master switch. There could be only one thing for it: I made sure all the boxes were illuminated.

With just one finger they were all off. Then they were all on again. The tubes inside had obviously started to get warm as they were coming on far more quickly than they had at first. I switched them all off again.

Then on. Off. On. Off. On. Off, on, off. Onoffonoff. It was then that I had a stroke of genius. If I held one side of the rocker on the switch down and pummelled the other side I could achieve new dizzy heights of flicker. It was like being at a one-man rave.

I got fed up and went to sit back on the bed. The clock on the wall showed I had used up all of fourteen minutes in my exploration of the X-ray boxes. There was nothing else for it: I was going to have to venture outside my room and go to the day room. Ten minutes later I was back lying on my bed.

An operating gown was delivered by a rosy-cheeked and portly nurse. She issued instructions at the speed of light and left the room, the smell of lunch pouring in through the briefly opened door. My stomach growled. And I felt particularly vulnerable wearing a large piece of paper with an opening up the back that was just crying out for a bit of unintended arse-flashing.

While pondering the fashion flaws of my operating gown and feeling the first tugs of apprehension about the impending operation, Dad turned up. A chrome-plated, wheelchair soon turned up as well, to ferry me to the operating theatre. 'Do you need help to get into the chair?' its driver asked in a stoop, expecting a positive response. 'Na, I'll be OK.'

I set about manoeuvring. I had difficulty cradling my right arm and holding the back of the gown closed to spare the attendant a look at my bum. I failed dismally, lost my grip of the gown, flashed my arse, then banged my arm against my side, which shot a searing pain through its length. I crashed onto, rather than sat in, the chair and all three of us set about sorting the foot rests. Quickly realising it was a solo task, Dad sat back on the bed and I sat back in the chair ready to be wheeled to theatre.

Glug. Silence . . . Whirr. Bleep bleep. Glug. Silence . . . Hiss. Evolving hiss. A modulating hiss. The anaesthetic was wearing off and I managed to open my eyes to glimpse various machines. All bleeped, chirped or burped their own song. Some with tubes, some with stick-on pads, most attached to me. Then I saw Mum sitting on a high-backed chair. She was smiling. I smiled back and passed out.

I woke next in my hospital bed, more lucid but thirsty and unable to get the sweet, spicy smell of the anaesthetic out of my nostrils. Some peculiar looking lollipop-sticks with miniature white sponges on their ends were upended in a cup next to a jug of water on the bedside cabinet.

'I really need a drink.' I said, making a tacky 'tut' between each word. 'The nurse said that you're allowed to just wet your lips with these things and then, if you're OK with that, you can have small sips. Any more and you'll be sick.'

Mum reached for the little lollipops and it was soon clear that water could be smuggled to my dehydrated innards by immersing the little sponges in water and then simply sucking the water from them. After several trips from cup to mouth, the sponge stick was laid to rest and I felt I was going to chuck. Mum peddled the usual 'Well you were told not to' vocabulary.

Poking and prodding

Later I counted my stitches. Rather impressed to find seventeen squashed into a fairly small wound at the top of my right shoulder, I stroked the neat fishing-line knots as they lay in an orderly line.

As I prodded the top of my right arm apprehensively, the skin felt almost rubbery. The expected influx of pain failed to materialise, giving the green light for probing to continue. Underneath the skin, just above the upper end of the wound, there was a tiny metal nodule. This was the top of the pin that reunited the disconnected pieces of bone. After watching intently, Mum was unable to restrain herself and started poking and prodding too.

We sat, played some cards and flicked the telly on. Flicked the telly off, got bored with cards. Then Dad and my younger brother Magnus (whom I called Mag) arrived. They filled us in on the unimportant goings-on of home in their complete entirety. That filled all of two and a half minutes. The conversation quickly turned towards David Bartley and the action that had been taken.

'He's been suspended for a couple of days, and I've

got a meeting with his father.' Dad spoke with an offi-
cious tone as if we were in the war rooms at Whitehall.
I was in a different frame of mind. I wanted to pull
the troops out, bring the navy into port and bury all the
explosives along with my head in the sand. With that
thought I responded, 'Oh.' Why didn't I care what
happened to him? Why didn't I want him to be
suspended for longer, get expelled or have a small penis
emerge from his forehead? Actually, a small dick growing
out of his forehead would be very amusing, but I wasn't
interested in the other stuff. It all seemed so harsh. My
eyes must have glazed over because the subject was
dropped and we were back to playing cards. The evening
drew in and it wasn't long before the three of them
had to leave.

Dad was obviously in constant communication with
the Bartley family and so at visiting time I would get
a daily roundup of events. It was all pretty much the
same. He was suspended *and* he was truly very sorry
and the other kids at school had ostracised him. The
last part of these little-changing updates was the only
part that gave me pause for thought. I had seen schoolyard persecution first-hand. It isn't pretty.

Dad came to see me midmorning on the third day
to tell me that my form tutor, Mrs Rowland, had asked
if I would like some of my friends to come and visit.
He had also come to tell me that David Bartley wanted
to come by. Although I wanted to pass the time, I
wasn't that keen to see my friends. It was really odd.

In hospital I was in small cocoon away from anyone connected with the event. With that comes the luxury of not having to explain the explained, a dislocation from confrontation. Paradoxically, the thought of seeing David Bartley was quite appealing. I wanted to say to him, 'Look at this, you idiot. *You* did this. Engage your tiny brain the next time you think about driving someone else's face into the dirt.' Perhaps something with a bit more sting that would stay with him for ever.

How could I say no to seeing my friends? With regard to David Bartley's appearance, Dad was less than enthusiastic. He kept saying, 'You know you don't have to.' But I *did* want to. I was seeing a mixture of anger, anguish and vengeance in Dad's eyes. He refrained from saying what he thought. It was to be my choice. I said no to a visit from Bartley. I've regretted it ever since.

Dr James's visits to my room were becoming more frequent. With each visit we were getting to know each other better. We talked about what had happened to me and how I felt; on rare occasions we would talk about him. I was fascinated by things he had done and places he had been. He would tell me pieces of information that other doctors and nurses would shy away from. There seemed an air of conspiracy, fuelling inklings that there was a much wider picture evolving out in the corridor – another world in comparison with my information-free microcosm. Dr James mentioned the possibility of a visit to a London hospital with increasing frequency. With a feeling of foreboding growing, I became fretful.

The visits from Mum, Dad and Mag carried on as usual. Any anxieties Mum and Dad were experiencing were expertly masked. I was on the lookout for any sort of clue while at the same time not wanting to know.

X-ray alarm

One day both Mum and Dad turned up in the middle of the afternoon. They entered the room with a doctor I'd seen only a few times, with Dr James in tow. The doctor looked unwaveringly into my eyes. A warm penetrating look on his face dulled the rat-a-tat-tat of the machine-gun words: 'You're going to have to go to London to have some tests. It's just routine. We'd like you to go because of this little fuzzy patch around the top of the bone on the X-ray.'

He duly jammed the film into the clasp and flicked the light on. 'It'll be OK,' I thought. 'What can a small fuzzy patch mean?' When I took photos myself they often had fuzzy bits. Various going-to-London noises were made by my parents and, with that, everyone filed out. It was a restless night's sleep for me.

As I've already said, my first trip to UCH inspired dread. It was hotly followed by my first chemotherapy session, a memorable day for all the wrong reasons.

Arriving in London, I had my overnight bag. It was light and I felt heavy. I was admitted and, shortly after, a drip stand appeared with a bag, filled with what looked like water, dangling from the top. Accompanying the drip stand was Dr Jonathon Shamash, and he looked as shattered as ever. In his hand, half hidden, he carried a small piece of pen-shaped, translucent plastic.

Before he opened his mouth I glanced at both of my parents, hoping for a final reprieve. None came. I was scared – of what, I wasn't sure. Uncertainty fed the monster eating away at me.

'This is a cannula,' said Dr Jonathon as he slid a thin needle with butterfly wings from its translucent package. 'It's a needle in a plastic tube,' he began to explain. I looked blank, hoping it might act as a delaying tactic. 'We'll put it in through the skin on your hand and then pull the needle out from the tube and connect you to the drip. Just a sharp scratch . . .' The needle had slid into a vein on the back of my hand smoothly but the square edge of the plastic tube sheathing it had no intention of going so quietly. The small vein on the back of my hand looked totally overwhelmed by the plastic juggernaut newly parked in it.

He slid the needle out leaving the tube embedded in the vein with a chunky plug taped to my wrist. From here the nurse took over. She attached a long clear tube to a saline bag hanging high above me to the plug of the cannula and twisted a small plastic tap mounted next to the plug. About halfway up the tube to the bag, a cigar-sized chamber allowed the drip to fall at a controlled rate. 'We're just putting saline into you now to keep the vein open.' The nurse smiled as she spoke. Her name badge said 'Sarah, Chemotherapy nurse' and she was beautiful.

It had all happened pretty quietly, this setting up. After the initial pain of having the cannula inserted, everything was ticking along fine. I was just beginning to think it was better than school when I glanced at my mum and dad. They looked shattered. As well as the anxiety that I'd often seen in previous days, there was the faintest hint of relief that treatment had started. I felt guilty and confused. There was more than one person going through this, yet only one person was going to beat it. That's right, isn't it? One person? Me?

Chemotherapy

Sarah entered the room with another bag of fluid, but this time it was covered by what looked like a red carrier bag. At full stretch, she hung it on the other arm of the stand and walked out again, only to reappear swiftly, holding a blue plastic box no bigger than a shoebox. She clamped it halfway up the stand with the kind of force that wrestlers usually reserve for one another. She plugged a power lead into the back and a small display on the front illuminated. The box made a curt beep, as if to acknowledge its rough treatment.

The first round of chemotherapy was mind-bending. After two hours I was violently sick. As day turned into night I tried to eat, but it just wouldn't stay down. I was asked to keep drinking, but I just couldn't. When visiting time finished, my parents had to leave. They didn't want to and it showed. I hope I never have to see either of them look that way again.

That first night all I yearned for was a mental void. I would get through one vomit convulsion with just enough time to brace for the next, feeling hot and cold and pouring with sweat. That night I fought for every single second. It was the most physically demanding time of my life.

At the end of forty-eight hours the first course had finished. Despite my aching body, I felt surprisingly upbeat. The recovery process had begun.

I had been away from home for a little over two days but it felt like much longer. My cat bounded over and stopped just in front of me. With all four paws planted firmly on the floor she looked up at me and meowed. Some people hate cats but I think they are fascinating. If she could have spoken she would have said, 'Giles, you may have a potentially life-threatening disease but I would like some Meow Mix this instant.' There's no point in wallowing when there's a cat around.

I was amazed that my hair remained intact. After two days I still felt fine, a little bit shaky but well enough to go back to school, and the following week that was exactly what I did. Upon my arrival, everyone was asking how I was. It was such a great feeling. In the fickle teenage world I inhabited I guessed this was what it must feel like to be cool. Older kids whom I didn't know talked to me as if I were someone they looked up to. I went to registration and lasted through my first lesson, and was then called to the office. I was sent home. I'd lasted just under two hours of the day.

When you're thirteen and someone takes something away from you, all you want to do is get it back. I felt as if I were being tossed onto the scrapheap by the school.

Every Friday my dad and I drove up to UCH for a blood test. Chemotherapy in its crudest sense is a way of flooding the body with nasty metals, which poison pretty much everything. The idea is that the tumour is the most sensitive body part and so dies more quickly than everything else. But the chemo was also pummelling my immune system, in particular my white blood cells. We had tried going to a local hospital and getting the results phoned through but the results had got lost. UCH had phoned up in a panic, so we decided to go all the way in to London each week.

After three weeks it was time for another dose. I was petrified. The smell of the place, the humid stale air and the filthy sticky floor flagged up what was about to happen: the sting of the cannula needle, the cold burn of the fluid coursing through my veins and the dread of the sickness to come. The dose was supposed to be slightly smaller but I couldn't tell the difference.

I was unaware at the time, but behind the scenes a pitched battle was raging between Mrs Marsham, the head at Chelmer Valley High, and my parents. As a child with cancer, I caused administrative problems. In short, even on the days when my white-blood-cell count was good, I was unable to go to school. My school work was on the slide in a big way and the door to fixing this problem was closed.

Convalescence

I was at home on my own most days. Mum and Dad were at work and my brother at school. I lasted about five weeks before something inside me seemed to implode. This was the first time I had ever felt true loneliness and it gripped me like a vice. I tried pacing around the house, but after a while I went to my bedroom, put my head into my pillow and cried. I cried until I was out of tears.

Dad came home to my misery. We agreed that it would be a good idea to invite some of my schoolfriends round for some pizza and video.

When hiring the video I made the same odd decision as I had when I first purchased a music tape. I found the one I really wanted – and then picked the one next to it. With music, Madonna's *True Blue* had been bumped by Mel and Kim's *FLM*, an album released in 1987 that was essentially one song remixed eleven times. In fact, even at the time, the singer Melanie Appleby was fighting her own cancer battle. She died of pneumonia while suffering spinal cancer in 1990, aged twenty-three. She did a television interview with Terry Wogan while she was incredibly ill. With her wicked sense of humour she was so positive and bubbly. When I went into hospital I took the tape. Just seeing her face on the cover was an inspiration.

Instead of choosing some fighting film that every teenage boy would want to watch in the video shop, I moved one to the left and picked up *Warlock*. It was rubbish – upon that, Kevin, Adam, Stuart and I were agreed.

But it was great to see them and we did a lot of laughing. However, I could see they were puzzled. I was laughing and joking, I looked just the same and I seemed in high spirits.

As the film drew to a close and we ran out of ways to mock it, I leaned back and rubbed my head. The evidence they perhaps sought was finally there. I looked down at my hand and saw a great clump of hair. That may well have been the first time that I saw some of my friends beyond their capacity to react appropriately to something like this in someone they knew. Even so, the evening was just what I needed and I felt a lot happier. Later on I was sitting in the bath, washing my hair. Eyes tight shut, I dunked my head under to rinse off. When I opened my eyes the water was full of hair. I've got very thick hair and, although the bathwater was thick with the stuff, there was no evidence of bald patches on my head. So, by the clump, I pulled it all out. Perhaps it sounds bizarre but I found it a liberating experience, finally to look like a cancer patient.

School was out but the swimming pool wasn't, and although I didn't get in it was great to go down to the pool and be with friends. People seemed so much more accepting there than anywhere else. It was nowhere near as good as doing it, but watching other people swimming gave me a connection with the water.

The third weekend session of chemotherapy was more of the same. It was the final dose before moving to the Royal National Orthopaedic Hospital (RNOH) in Stanmore, on the outskirts of north London. According to figures from a new charity called the Teenage Cancer Trust (TCT), one in 330 boys and one in 420 girls will contract cancer before their twentieth birthday. Teenagers get some of the most aggressive cancers, exacerbated by their growth spurts.

If you can imagine sneezing onto a piece of paper and then using that as the basis of a blueprint for a building, then you would probably come fairly close to the footprint of the RNOH. No building went higher than the first floor and the entire group of buildings that made up the hospital were built crazily on a hill. It was originally a hospital for highly contagious diseases, hence all the separate buildings. Over time they were connected with a series of covered corridors. This was definitely design by evolution, not revolution. I was due to check into Colonel Wood Ward.

Walking in it was like something from science fiction. There were about twenty teenagers on beds connected to all kinds of weird and wonderful gadgets: there were people in plastic body moulds for correcting spinal curvature; some had precise metal structures around legs to lengthen shortened limbs; others had the full overhead cradle with various limbs suspended by weights on pulleys. The nurses' station was at one end where the ward joined onto Lionel Williams Ward. That was full of teenagers, too, though they were all older.

Shattered dreams

We checked in and a nurse showed me to my bed. I sat on it with my parents and we looked at each other blankly. About an hour passed and still nothing. A polite doctor arrived and introduced himself, drawing the curtain round the bed. I took my T-shirt off automatically; it was pretty obvious what he'd come to see. The small head of the steel pin that was holding my broken arm together could just be seen under the surface of my skin. He got me to stand up and raise my arm forward as far as I could. I did and it went to pretty much exactly 90 degrees horizontal. He then asked me to reach up laterally as high as I could. With my arm lifted from the side it again went to 90 degrees horizontal. What he said next will be seared into my memory until I die. With a casual glance at the chart board he said saw some of my friends beyond their capacity 'That'll probably be the limit of your shoulder movement after the operation. OK?' He smiled at Mum, drew back the curtain and was gone. I just couldn't believe it. With one sentence my Olympic dream disappeared.

I looked at Mum and I think she had guessed something like that was coming. I was heartbroken and grasped her wrists as if I were clutching at straws. I couldn't think of a single thing to say, except 'But . . .'

Practically everyone there had some kind of mobility problem but I was able to wander round and, because everyone was around my age, it was pretty good fun. People were in there for long periods of time and so a whole raft of schoolteachers came in. There were even ward romances in which lovesick teens would send each other messages. It was the first time that I really noticed women. Some of the nurses on the ward were incredible. These weren't girls: they were proper women.

Every so often the 'Nil by mouth' sign would appear and a bed with its occupant would disappear. It wasn't long before I was woken at 4 a.m. and offered some dry toast as the sign went up above my bed. My parents both arrived that morning and sat on my bed. I was tucked in so tightly I felt as if I were bound in sheet steel. A wisecracking nurse called Sylvia came to give me an injection; from then on I was sky high. As they wheeled me in my bed through the double doors and outside into the rain onto the main slope, I wanted to get of bed and help the porter push. Sylvia had come too and was joking all the way, but she turned the humour down as we rounded a corner of the shack-like corridor and moved through the operating-theatre doors.

The operating theatres were right in the centre of all the buildings and, in contrast to the other tired-looking structures, were like something from another world. Every surface shone brilliantly. We stopped in a small room and through a window in the door I could see the empty operating theatre gleaming. It was extra-ordinarily stark: a grey floor with white tiles floor to ceiling and a huge operating lamp that hung in the centre of the room like a gigantic insect poised to pounce.

The engineer who had made the prosthesis, the metal bone that was to replace my humerus, arrived. Shortly after, Mr Cannon the surgeon appeared. He was a mountain of a man and had that air of confidence you really need from anyone who wields a scalpel. I asked him if I could have the pin from my arm once he had removed it. I got a 'maybe' nod. He checked I was OK and then it was over to the anaesthetist. I counted backwards from one hundred . . .

I woke up in intensive care, my right arm immobilised next to my body, wrapped in tight bandages. I felt disgusting. But I knew what to expect from the previous operation and so decided to drink too much water with the inevitable consequences. I spent a groggy night there before being moved back to Colonel Wood.

My imagination ran riot over what my arm might look like under the bandages. When they came off for the first time I was relieved to see that it looked a lot better than I had envisaged. It was incredibly swollen with a huge corkscrew scar twisting down from the front of my shoulder to under my elbow. Rather than stitches there were eighty-nine metal staples running its length. Somewhere inside my arm was a lump of titanium a foot long. I couldn't help but be amazed at what had happened while I was asleep.

Road to recovery

As soon as I was able to engage in the ward's social shenanigans, I was well enough to study and soon I was being sent down to the physiotherapy department once a day for an hour-and-a-half session. I was being treated by the head of physiotherapy. He was a wonderful guy with a thick Indian accent and a name that I just couldn't get right. Instead I called him Fizz, which tickled him. The exercises he got me to do were incredibly challenging.

The shoulder is made up of a series of muscle groups. The largest ones, the deltoids, hang down over the shoulder like a bunch of bananas. These power the movement of the arm from the shoulder. Underneath these are a series of smaller muscles that make up a complex called the rotator cuff, and it is their job to hold the shoulder in place. Part of my anterior deltoid, the banana that lifts the arm forward, had been removed in the operation in order to get the bone out and the prosthesis in. The problem was that it had scrambled my nerve endings. I kept accessing movement of my rotator cuff muscles – in essence I was producing movement but it was slow, the tiny muscles trying to lift the weight of my arm. Occasionally I would get it right and my arm would move much more quickly, but it took every last volt of thought to do it. The frustration was offset by Fizz's elation when I'd activated the right muscle group.

After three weeks of recovery and intensive physio I was all set to be discharged. It was both exciting and disheartening. It was going to be great to get back into the world, but it also meant restarting chemo for the final three sessions. I had started to feel really well again, almost healthy, and thought of going back to the nightmarish Private Patients Ward Two was not an appealing one.

My parents had won the battle with the school and, when I felt OK, I could go in on one condition: that I wasn't outside during break times. Instead, I had to go to the school nurse's room. Mrs Rowland, my form tutor, organised a rota between friends who could come and keep me company. It was a nice thought but I didn't want to stop someone else from having their break just because I couldn't have mine. But I could make up for this shortcoming in classes. The teachers all gave me a lot more latitude than most and I would be very cheeky to get a laugh. I knew I was playing the clown but just didn't care. This was a new escapism.

When I couldn't make it in to school I had home tutors. By far the best was Touchi Kalsee; everyone called him Touch. He had lived in the UK for many years but had grown up in Kenya, although his family's roots were in India. With his warm, rounded voice he always knew the exact way to phrase something to make it come alive. He taught me maths and with him the numbers were like characters with their own personalities. Within a short space of time I had easily caught up the ground I had lost at school.

The chemotherapy was still reducing in dose with each visit, but now I could actually discern the difference. My immune system wasn't being pushed so hard, which was reflected in the weekly blood tests. More than once I had recorded a white-blood-cell count so low that it had delayed everything. Six weeks after the operation and with chemo Round Four out of the way, I went back to RNOH to have the staples taken out of my 14-inch scar. Sylvia was there to do it and was armed with a small pair of crimpers. They were really quite ingenious: two small prongs went between the staple and the skin with one over the top; when she squeezed the handle, the single prong pushed a V into the staple as it tried to move between the two on the other side. Most of the staples just came out but some had become a bit grown over and were a bit tricky. As Sylvia went carefully down the scar removing staples, she told this story (if you try to imagine it read by Jane Horrocks you'll be fairly close).

Once upon a time in Purple Land, there was a purple man. One morning in Purple Land he got up and looked out of the window of his purple house at his purple car. It sat under the purple tree, which had big round purple fruit on it.

He got out of his purple pyjamas and had a shower using purple soap. He got dressed in his purple suit and went to work in his purple office. When he arrived there he got some purple paper and began to fill out order forms for more purple. Purple bricks for people's purple houses, purple purses for purple ladies' purple purchases and all kinds of purple peculiarities besides.

When it got to lunchtime the purple man went down the purple stairs of the purple office to by some purple sandwiches. As he walked out of the purple door another man all in purple put a purple pouch in his purple paw and ran off along the purple pavement. Bewildered, our purple man just stood there, unsure what to do.

He looked up and down the purple pavement but

the purple man had gone. He looked inside the purple pouch to see that it was full of purple pounds. That's when the purple police pulled up and arrested him for perpetrating the purple peculiarity with the Purple Pimpernel!

They took him to the purple police station and took his purple fingerprints, walked him down a purple corridor to a purple door. The purple policeman took out a big bunch of purple keys and opened the purple door and do you know what he said?

By this point both my dad and I were in hysterics and on the edge of our seats desperate for her to tell us.

'In-di-go!' said Sylvia, triumphantly holding the last staple. I hadn't felt a thing.

Eventually I returned to the pool. It was a great feeling being back in the water again and my coach Ann was getting the balance just right, challenging me but not pushing too hard. I was still in chemo, had no hair and got tired very easily, but I was weary of being mollycoddled. Other kids at swimming club just got on with it. I could use my right arm a bit but I had to swim using mainly just my left. I had lost all of my fitness and consequently swam pretty slowly. If I was in the way they told me and that was how I wanted it. At swimming club I didn't have to be the clown because I was happy being me.

I couldn't believe the sixth and final chemo session:

it was so easy. I wasn't being sick and the sun was coming in through the window on a bright weekend in the spring of 1990. It was the start of a new decade. I'd been to hell and back and I could just sit there and think about all the great things I was going to do with my life.

I watched the final few drops of the chemo bag drain into the cannula tube and down into my left wrist. I shouted for Sarah to come in and take 'all this rubbish down'. She was in the room in a flash and had a big grin. 'You're done!' she said as she disconnected me. I leaped out of bed and quickly started packing up. 'Aren't you going to get dressed?' asked Mum.

'Nope.' I was desperate to get out of there. But I did have to get dressed. We got in the car and headed home.

Chapter Four

Cancer Revisited

At school my celebrity status dwindled as my hair grew. All the same old hierarchies that existed before were still there. I didn't want to be part of them but I was soon entrenched once again; everyone was.

Swimming club, as ever, was different. Perhaps it is just a romantic memory but people seemed much more at ease with themselves there. I started training in the early mornings again, to my immense joy. My Olympic dreams were well and truly on the cutting-room floor. But I had other ideas. I could be a rock star. I had always loved music but now I really started to notice it. I wasn't alone and the swimming club became a music-swapping shop. Rarely a week went by without a new band appearing on the radar.

I was happy just getting back into life. I was coming to the end of my fourth year at Chelmer Valley High, which meant just one more year until my GCSE exams.

School was going well. Swimming had moved into the realm of hobby rather than sport. It was becoming a social club for many rather than a group of people with a common goal. I was coasting along, having managed to put the brakes on every area of change I could think of. I was tired of change. During chemotherapy it had been all I'd known, from my physical or emotional condition to the way people reacted to me. Looking back, I realise it was my black-and-white approach that was a problem. My weariness and fear of change had led me to the knee-jerk reaction of halting all change. It had killed my Chimo Cycle when what I needed to do was to change to smaller *increments* of change to keep it alive.

On 19 October 1987, more than a quarter of the value of shares listed on the London Stock Exchange disappeared in just over a couple of hours. It became known as Black Monday and it was the catalyst for the spiralling global recession that reached everyone. It just seemed to be one bad news story after another in the professional lives of my parents' friends. In the summer of 1991 Dad was made redundant. It was a beautiful day and we sat in the garden. Dad was pensive but upbeat and, as a family, we brainstormed ideas for all sorts of things.

The company car had gone and cash was tight, but Dad decided he needed transport and bought an old pimple-dented Honda Civic for £500. He worked on it and got it running well, arguably too well. It had phenomenal acceleration but there simply wasn't enough fuel coming out of the North Sea to keep it happy. We were able to zip in and out of traffic like a tiny insect. This, coupled with its inefficiency, quickly earned it the affectionate title of the Squanderbug, and it became the wheels for Dad's new company, Bruce Long Design.

The school had tried to push me out of the top set for maths, but I had managed to fight this battle myself and it turned out to be a good move – if only because it made me realise, if only in part, that you didn't have to be riddled with disease in order for people to listen to you. It just took a well-constructed argument.

Second time around

It was a Sunday lunchtime training session at Braintree pool. The summer sunlight was streaming in through giant south-facing windows. Only five of us turned up and Dad was coaching the session. We stood on the poolside getting our gear together. Dad wrote out the warm-up and set us to start on red-top – when the red needle of the pace clock hits 12 o'clock. Just as we were about to start he took hold of my arm and said sharply, 'Is that OK?' He was looking at a large red patch on my right arm just below the shoulder. It appeared hot but felt fairly cool to the touch and I was fine. I dismissed it saying, 'Mr Cannon said the metal would reflect heat in a different way from bone. It's probably just got hot in the sun.'

As a safety precaution I went to the RNOH. Mr Cannon was there with several of his students. There was no messing about that day. It was civil but purely business. I felt uneasy. He said he wanted a biopsy, with the results copied to him and Professor Souhami at UCH, who was organising the chemotherapy. Professor Souhami was rated by many as being one of the best in the world and was consequently a very busy man. Mr Cannon said goodbye, shook my hand and left. They must have thought it was urgent, because we made an appointment to come back in two days.

We did go back, and were shown into one of the dressing rooms attached to the Colonel Wood Ward. With a needle as thick as a drinking straw, Mr Cannon's senior house officer performed the biopsy. It didn't hurt a bit, just created a strange vibration as metal needle hit metal bone. After ten minutes it was done. I had a puncture wound the diameter of a small pea at the top of my right arm, which was then dressed; shortly after, we were on the road and home in just over an hour. I got my stuff and we went to the pool.

Several days later, Mum and I were at home. It was a blustery and chilly day. Although the heating was on I was shivering and I decided to have a sleep in the afternoon. I wrapped myself tightly with the duvet and that seemed to work. But at around seven I started warming up. Then I just couldn't cool down. I began pouring with sweat and became delirious. The fever had been so intense over the short period that I couldn't stand. I don't know how, but Mum carried me downstairs and put me in the car.

I woke up at Broomfield Hospital just outside Chelmsford, Essex. I was in a large modern room, quite different from the austere panelling of UCH. I was on my own for about two minutes of consciousness when the door flew open to reveal an old lady with frizzy flyaway hair. 'Have you seen my frying pan?' she proclaimed. She wandered over to the wardrobe, politely introducing herself as Joan on the way, and then proceeded to throw everything out of it in search of the missing pan. Eventually, a nurse appeared and steered her out of the room.

I was in Broomfield for just a night. Once my temperature was under control, I was given a prescription and discharged. But a new black dawn was just over the horizon.

Within days I was back at the Royal National Orthopaedic with Dad. We met the towering Mr Cannon and his senior house officer on Colonel Wood. Mr Cannon showed us into the day room just off the ward. The house officer stayed outside. For the first time ever, this confident man looked burdened. 'I'm afraid it's back,' he said.

There were chairs, but all three of us were standing. Dad and I were silent. 'To make matters worse, it's become infected.' He put a hand to his brow and drew breath. 'The tumour has recurred. It's wrapped itself partially around the head of the prosthesis and this has become infected. That's what caused your temperature.'

He looked at me and his face lifted, though almost imperceptibly. A confidence of tone returned to his voice. We were on to the options and this is where Steve Cannon knew his stuff. He continued, 'When there's problem within the body, it attacks from all sides. It contains it. But this infection is pressed up against the prosthesis, giving your immune system only one front from which to attack it. Then there's the problem of the tumour. That will need more chemotherapy.'

There was a protracted pause. 'You can have the arm amputated and be done with it or you can have the chemotherapy and the operations and you may still lose your arm at the end of it. What do you want to do?'

'Well, I've got to fight, haven't I?' I said, through lips of stone.

'Is that what you want to do?' Dad asked.

'If I don't, I'll always wonder "what if?"'

'You have to realise we're fighting fire with fire here,' said Mr Cannon. 'We're at the very limits. Are you absolutely sure?' It was the final time of asking. I nodded. I gave a deep sigh and Dad said, 'We really thought we were out of the woods on this one.'

'I know, Mr Long.'

Mr Cannon put a hand on each of my shoulders and smiled saying, 'Well, it *is* the right arm, I suppose.' I'd have been prepared to do the same for the left. But

I liked the fact that he was able to have a joke in a situation like that. Dad and I drove home in the Squanderbug and prepared for battle.

Battle lines drawn

The surprise of change being thrust upon you is terrifying. Perhaps the biggest mistake I could have made would have been to decide a course of action straightaway. Instead, I allowed myself to be scared for a bit before deciding what changes were going to happen and how I could turn them to my advantage. I was fighting for my right arm, and what could be more motivating than that? But it amazes me, looking back, how such negative news started another Chimo Cycle.

We'd asked Mr Cannon if going swimming so close to having had the biopsy could have been the cause of the infection. He said not, but I have occasionally wondered if he said that because there would have been no point in saying otherwise. Sometimes the only battle worth looking at is the one in front. What's the point of attributing blame if all you're looking for is a bit of scenery?

We came back a few days later to hear the plan of action. It was going to be another six rounds of chemotherapy: three pre-operation, three post-operation. But this time there would be *operations* – plural. The first would be to remove the prosthesis and replace it with a 'bio-stick', a plastic tube coated in a powerful penicillin. That would be left in for six weeks to kill the infection. It would then be removed and replaced with a new prosthesis, made of two parts. The top half was a temporary 'spacer' to stabilise the shoulder and was to be looked at in the future. The bottom half was essentially a hinge, which would act as an elbow joint.

'With each operation you lose something, and I'm afraid that will mean the remaining use of your right shoulder, Giles.' Mr Cannon was clear as ever. Warm but clear.

That night I found a small space to be by myself. It wasn't important which room, just that it was confined, dimly lit and contained. I took a small mirror with me and looked into it and said these words quietly but aloud: 'You know what this means and you know what you have to do. But this will be the last time. If you can hear me in there, you little fucker, I want you to know that I won't let you take me a piece at a time. You have to live in me and if you won't go then I will. Then you'll die too. So come on, show me what you've got. Come on.'

It felt like war. There we were – I, my family, my friends, my doctors, my nurses – on one side and cancer on the other. I had been to see Professor Souhami again and he had a look of grim determination on his face from the moment I walked through the door. The first time around, there had been several occasions when I'd woken up late in the evening with him just standing at the end of my bed. Those times he looked as smart as if he'd just arrived for work in the morning.

We were always joking and I was always cheeky – he always had students with him and loved it when I referred to them as his disciples. I gave him a birthday card one year, just as I was leaving a check-up. In it I'd written, 'I bet you thought there'd be money in it!' He came running down the corridor after me and proclaimed in front of everyone there, 'You're too stingy to put any money in it!' He was right: I was.

He tried to keep his distance from his patients but he cared so much about what he did that I think he never managed to wholly sever his professional life from his personal. That day in his office there were no jokes, just the occasional weak smile, as he explained how the show was going to roll from a chemotherapy angle. I knew what was coming and was dreading it.

Changes

As before the whole thing seemed to get started a lot more quickly than I'd anticipated. Though there were some changes. This time I was going to the Middlesex Hospital not far from UCH in the heart of London. There was a new kind of ward there, which had been set up by the TCT. When we arrived at the Middlesex and walked in, it looked in slightly better shape than UCH, but retained that feeling of

Victorian austerity. The hospital-food smell seemed to seep out of the beige walls and floor. We wandered through a maze of corridors and took the lift to the second floor, to the Teenage Cancer Trust Ward. The doors opened to a bright vibrant space. If a sound-track had been needed it would have simply said, 'Hallelujah!'

No one was in uniform and above my bed was a huge Happy Mondays poster. There was a day room that you might actually want to spend some time in, stocked with games, videos, albums and books. The patients, although hairless, seemed at ease. What was going on? I put my things in my bedside cabinet and nervously waited for the nurse to come and start the whole process again.

The cannula hurt as badly as it had before and the drip bag once again chilled me to the core. I awaited the vomiting and convulsions with deep-seated fear. But the ambient surroundings were a distraction. Even the most ill person in the room seemed to be having nothing more than a light doze. There were even two patients playing table tennis in the middle of the small ward. Where was all the gloom?

As my first bag of chemotherapy went up the answer presented itself in the form of a tiny white pill. This was ondansetron, an anti-sickness drug that had come onto the market since my first chemo course. As far as I'm concerned, it's one of the greatest inventions ever. Each little white pill cost £15 and I can't remember how many I had each day, but at the time I would have given a tooth for each one.

So no vomiting and convulsions this time. I didn't feel great, but could wander around, chat to people, read and do all the things you would do at home. This time my outlook was on a higher plane altogether. I genuinely couldn't believe that this was all supposed to cure the same thing. When I got home my body ached and I got tired easily, but my recovery time after each session was far shorter.

But it was clear that I was being sheltered from a lot of the other problems around. Interest rates were in double figures and Mum and Dad had to cope with a mortgage that was going up when the recession just kept biting. Healthcare in the UK may be free but everything that goes with it is not. Weekly trips to hospitals for blood tests and X-rays all ate cash. The Squanderbug had broken down for the final time and had to be replaced. The school was more on side this time and I could go in when I felt able. It was my final year leading up to my GCSEs and I had home tutors again, but sadly couldn't get the local authority to pay for Touch. My parents found the money from somewhere for me to see him privately.

I was assigned two different tutors by the local authority; Ursula and Dr Putnam. Unfortunately, Ursula specialised in history, German and art. I had taken geography over history and French over

German. Dr Putnam, however, was much more like Touch. He was a retired scientist and really loved the subject. I can't ever remember writing a thing down with him. It was always a discussion followed by questions. Most of what he taught me I can remember today.

Collateral damage

Just after the second chemo session I became aware for the first time of the effect that the whole thing was having on Mag. With the family's resources angled at getting me better, the toll on him was enormous. I had to make a lot of hard decisions for myself but I had lots of people around me to support me. He was making hard decisions every day on his own and one night I heard him crying in his room.

When I started writing this book he told me how, in that period, he saw Mum cry for the first time. Prior to that he had not fully realised the gravity of the whole saga. But, seeing her weeping in the lounge, he made a conscious decision to bury his feelings of jealousy and envy. He turned out to be the big man and is an unsung hero of the story.

Ondansetron was not only allowing me to do more days at school but also to go swimming. It was a place I still loved to be. I could get new music there and listen to it on my Walkman when I was in hospital.

School had swung the other way. The celebrity status wasn't present this time and, although people I didn't know in the school seemed to have an air of understanding about them, people in my form and my year started actively to question my illness. On top of that, David Bartley became a hero – the logic being that if he hadn't broken my arm I would be dead, never mind the fact that his actions had cost me my entire humerus instead of a small part of it: it had to go, because there was a danger of knocking cancer cells from the affected top to the unaffected bottom. It was hardly grounds for heroism but arguing the point was futile.

With three chemo sessions completed, the tumour was responding well. Again, I had no hair but I felt so much better than I had done the first time around. The staff at the TCT Ward were all brilliant and I can honestly say that at times it came close to being enjoyable. But the chemo halfway mark meant going back up to the Royal National Orthopaedic in Stanmore for the operations.

I was looking forward to getting them done. I'd been taking a cocktail of pills daily to keep the infection at bay and my veins were starting to collapse all over the place from the chemo. When I got to the RNOH, I went to the isolation ward at the top of the crazy slope. After checking in, I got shown to my room. The building was prefabricated but I had a TV, a big window, even my own kettle. Amazing! I was a teenager with my own pad.

Out with the old

After a few days of prep I was in for the operation: prosthesis out, bio-stick in. I was an old hand at it now. I got back to my room and lay there. Tapped fingers and lay there. Watched television, read a bit and listened to music. Whenever a nurse came in she had to dress in a sterile disposable apron and wear a mask, so did the teachers from Colonel Wood ward.

I had an inspirational teacher, Mrs Smith, an Australian. She made me love English and seemed to have a way of bringing texts alive – the art of good teaching. But after two weeks in that small room I began to struggle. I was scheduled to be on the isolation ward for six weeks. I was in prison when I hadn't done anything wrong. I knew I had to stay and give the bio-stick the absolute best chance of working, but I couldn't help trading with myself in my mind. I started having ridiculous thoughts such as, 'How much is my right arm worth? A trip to the shops? Maybe a little bit more? Maybe less?' It was becoming a psychological fight above all else. My family came as often as they could, but visits that could be measured in minutes left a lot of lonely hours.

On 23 December 1991 Mr Cannon said that I could go home for Christmas. I could have kissed him.

This was my final year of high school. I had a big operation and load of chemo to go before I could even think about getting to the exams. Fairly soon I was back on the Lionel Williams ward and being prepped for my third big operation in eighteen months.

The operation was a success and very quickly I was back on the ward. Everything seemed to function a lot faster than it had the first time. It had been a test of endurance for Mr Cannon: I'd been on the operating table for just under five hours and lost five pints of blood.

I'd had a lot of transfusions while I was under anaesthetic but I've only ever had one while I was conscious. Sylvia put a bag on a drip stand with 'A+' printed on a yellow sticker. 'Once you've had this you'll feel all alive and awake,' she said. I did.

This time physiotherapy was much less intense. There was just so much less to work on. Strengthening my biceps, triceps and hand was about all there was to do. But less time spent in the physio department was what I needed. I had to hit the books. If I wasn't going to make it as a swimmer I had better make sure I got a good education.

I was transferred back to the TCT at the Middlesex for the final three chemo sessions. On the Saturday morning of my fifth chemo session one of the nurses wandered over to each of the beds, talking quietly to each patient individually. In the night a girl in one of the small rooms off the TCT Ward had died. I didn't know who she was but I felt a great loss. It was like losing one of the team to our common foe. Some people felt incredibly guilty that they were responding well to the chemo and she hadn't. Personally, it made me angry inside at the disease. I couldn't wait for that session to end and Mum stayed with me until 2 a.m., when the last drip bag finished, so that I could get out of there.

Touch and Dr Putnam both knew how the system worked and started coaching me to get through my GCSE exams. Chemo was wearing on and I was tired of being continually prodded and poked, needled and knifed. I would get down to the pool as much as I could but trying to apply myself to my school work as well as having chemo was exhausting. I missed all of my mock exams but Dr Putnam didn't seem too worried. Touch was a little more concerned and got hold of lots of past exam papers.

In March 1992 I finished my last chemotherapy session. I felt a tired bliss and crossed my fingers.

After a couple of days' rest I went back into school and slowly got back into swimming. Mike Gosling had been head coach at the swimming club for a couple of years and let me swim with the top squad even though I was too slow to be included. I moved through April trying to pick up what revision tips I could from classes at school. As the year got warmer, I had more time to look at the people around me. It was amazing how people had changed in such a short space of time. Their conversations all seemed a bit pointless. I'd met so many interesting people on my journey through hospital, and there'd been so many ideas and people that I wanted to emulate.

Dad dropped me off for my first exam. I remember feeling relatively calm but he said I was ringing my hands the whole way. It was geography, one of my favourite subjects, and I left feeling pretty good.

Once I hit the rhythm of sitting exams, they flew by. But when they were finished it was good riddance to school but for one final day – results day. On the 27 August 1992 I went to Chelmer Valley for the last time with both my parents. I left them in the car as I went inside to get my results. I sloped back to the car and quietly got in, holding the pieces of paper, sighed and pushed my forehead into my hand. Mum and Dad were both silent. They'd both hoped for the best but feared the worst. Mum slowly leaned around from the back seat and took the pieces of paper from me. About two seconds passed before she shouted at the top of her lungs, *'Oh my God I don't believe it!'* I'd got one A, and Bs in everything else.

Chapter Five

Being Disabled and Being Me

Coming to terms with my disability was like a gradual application for a passport. One of the things that frightened me the most about the title was that in some way I was entering a land that I could never leave. At first, I would dash in and dash out, get to training camps or competitions, do the swimming, and then leave as quickly as possible. Almost as if I stayed too long, I would turn to stone.

The teenage years are an uncertain time for everyone. Like those around me, I was struggling to work out what and who I was. I knew I had a disability and my family knew it too, but I could still walk down the street without anyone noticing. Even though my right arm is an inch and a half shorter than my left and my shoulders are a bit asymmetric, people rarely spot the differences, even if I'm wearing a T-shirt. This still surprises me today.

One day at school, one of boys came in with one of his eyebrows shaved off. No one noticed until he pointed it out, something he wished he hadn't done. But how often do you really look at people? So, if that's how most people are as they walk down the road, why would I want to rubber-stamp the fact that I've got a disability? I'm getting away with it! Or so I used to think. At the start I held disability sport at arm's length. But, inevitably, I would have to embrace the status. I did this later rather than sooner, partly because I had other challenges on my mind.

Only two people I knew from school moved on to my new college in Braintree. It was the chance for a new start that I wanted for so long. It was a gateway to whole new set of ideas. At Braintree Tertiary College I was in education, enjoying it and meeting new people of my age who I thought were ready to move on like me. The college had been newly built and moved to tertiary status from being a further-education college. This meant that it encompassed all of Braintree's pupils over the age of sixteen. Through teenage eyes I could see only one slight downside: Mum was a lecturer there.

The last domestic competition in the swimming season calendar is in late July – the National Championships. But 1992 was also Olympic year and the Barcelona games had been the most spectacular ever. There was some amazing British success on the track with Linford Christie winning the coveted 100 metres and Sally Gunnell taking the 400-metre hurdles. Chris Boardman rode a revolutionary bike and won at the velodrome; the Searle brothers won the coxed pairs; and sporting legend Steve Redgrave picked up his third gold. As it turned out, he was only halfway through his career.

In the first week of the games there had been both success and disappointment in the pool. Nick Gillingham had taken bronze in the 200-metre breast-stroke in a performance that suggested there was more to come in future games. Adrian Moorhouse was at his third games and defending the gold medal he had won by 0.01sec in the 100-metre breaststroke four years previous in Seoul. He finished in eighth place, still a significant achievement, though it had an additional dimension at Braintree & Bocking Swimming Club, where many remembered the great talent of Ian Mackenzie. He would have come of age in 1992. I couldn't help thinking it was all a terrible waste. How many potential Olympic medallists are walking the streets of Great Britain even as I type?

The Olympics drew to a close and were packed away for another four years. After a training session two weeks later I stood chatting to fellow swimmer Steve Wager on the poolside. He was telling me about something called the Paralympics. He said that maybe I should think about going for it but I dismissed it as some-thing for disabled people. And that wouldn't be me,

I thought with certainty. Like many others, I attached the 'Para' of the title to the word *paraplegic* rather than *parallel*.

By late September 1992, my hair was back to normal. The long scar down my right arm had faded from an angry red highway to a light-pink footpath and, apart from a bony shoulder, I looked perfectly healthy. I had laid the foundations for a new set of technical skills slowly over the previous two years, but I now had a chance to build my fitness and strength too. Mike Gosling was head coach at Braintree Swimming Club and passionate about the sport. When I reached the point when I could match the training pace of the other swimmers in the group, he started to enter me for competitions.

Pooling resources

Each competitive swimming event has its own personality. The brash zip of the 50-metre freestyle is completely different from the carnival feel of the relays, for example. But across the swimming programme there are three events that are recognised by most in the sport as the toughest: the 1,500-metre freestyle, the 400-metre individual medley and the 200-metre butterfly. At my first competitive swimming competition since I had been first diagnosed with cancer in 1989, Mike entered me in the 200-metre butterfly, not to drive me from the sport completely or to toughen me up, but because the harder events drew fewer competitors and the more undersubscribed they were the easier the qualifying time.

I got thrashed. I was swimming with one arm and everyone else was swimming with two. But when I finished every spectator applauded. My time of 2 minutes 48 seconds was slow but my personal-best book was now a blank canvas. I'd set myself a mark to beat next time.

There was a minute shift in my relationship with my peers at the swimming club. In doing just one swimming competition I had gone from 'sick Giles' back to 'Giles the swimmer'. It was subtle but I felt as if my being there had value again, that I was helping to support an ethos, rather have it support me. It was as if the individual Chimo Cycle of each member of the group was once again balanced by the effort exerted by each individual. The Chimo Cycle of the team was once again a wheel with all the spokes under correct tension.

Every day produced new surprises and at college I was making new friends all the time. In an early geography lecture I met Joey Gardiner. A tall man who loves music and is now an excellent jazz pianist, he is still one of my best friends today. We joined the Student Union executive together because a nice-looking girl asked us to. From then on we were relatively ineffectual in a relatively ineffectual organisation.

The swim meets kept coming, though they were

losing their appeal and becoming a bit puzzling and a chore. We would travel to the competition, I'd get beaten, people would applaud and we'd drive home. I knew that people were clapping to express encouragement or admiration. But I wasn't doing it for them. In the car on the way home from each competition I'd started to wonder whom I was doing it for. I was in limbo, no longer part of the sport I'd taken up nine years before, and, if there was something else out there, I was unaware of it and so wasn't part of that, either.

Autumn was turning to winter in 1992 and I decided that I wanted to carry on swimming, but not do the competitions. I put the idea to Mike. His response was simple: 'I have a team of people all working towards a common goal: to swim at their fastest at the end of each season. Each person here is trying to drive their own change and move forward. For that we all need to be motivated and the only way we can do that is if we think about the next big race. That's the only motivator we've got when it's early in the morning, cold and we've got to come down here [the pool]. The only way we can fuel that is to keep coming up with new ideas. One of the best ways to generate those is to keep changing things, no matter how small – stop competing and pushing to better your times and the sport will stagnate for you. Swimmers compete as individuals but we train as a team. You have to be part of that or the cycle that is driving the whole team will stop working.' The choice was clear: carry on competing and improve or quit. Although unaware of it, he was, in essence, the first person to spell out the Chimo Cycle to me.

In early 1993 I entered a swimming meet at Fullwell Cross in Ilford, east London. There had been some impressive times by junior swimmers tipped to go on to swim for Great Britain, though my performance had been fairly average. Beverly Gull, a Paralympian from Barcelona, was also there and saw me swim. I didn't get to meet her that day but she became a significant other person in my swimming career.

Paralympic glimpse

I joined an organisation called the Association of British Swimmers (ABS), a group of disabled swimmers who met once a month at the Stoke Mandeville Hospital. Ludwig Guttman, a neurologist working with Second World War veterans with spinal injuries, used sport in the rehabilitation programmes he set for his patients. He organised the first small-scale events of what would become the Parallel Olympics to coincide with the London competition in 1948. Soon it became known as the Paralympics.

At the Seoul games in 1988 the Paralympics was the biggest and best it had ever been. The tradition was maintained in Barcelona. At Stoke Mandeville it was interesting seeing where the games had first started, but each time I went I wasn't really sure why I was there.

We slept in large dormitories of ten that were like hospital wards. I'd spent just over two years in and out of hospital and now I was back in one. It didn't seem like fun.

It was Dad who kept encouraging my going to the ABS weekends. I think he saw that it might lead to something bigger, or perhaps he, too, just saw it as re-habilitation. After three training weekends we finally got to meet Beverley Gull.

She was a petite woman with short, blonde, curly hair, who pushed a wheelchair with fluorescent pink tubes. In her proud cockney accent she wasn't back-wards in coming forwards. Without preliminaries, she asked, 'So what's your problem? Born like it? Accident?' It was the first time I'd ever had to categorise what had happened and was completely at a loss for words. 'Er, cancer,' I said.

'Oh, trauma,' she said.

She then proceeded to tell me all the answers before I'd even had time to formulate the questions. It was almost spooky. What also came out of the conversation was an invitation to a training weekend in Darlington, where some of the Great Britain team would also be in action.

When I got home I looked on the map to see where Darlington was – 250 miles north of Braintree. Still, it was exciting to be asked to go and swim with such a high-calibre group, and two weeks later I was on the train from King's Cross heading north with Beverley.

We arrived at a large Victorian building, its heavy red brick serving as a reminder of the industrial wealth that must have once flowed through the town. I checked in and made my way through various winding stairways and along creaking corridors to my room. It was luxurious and a world away from the utilitarian décor at Stoke Mandeville.

I dumped my stuff on the floor next to the bed and made my way downstairs to the ballroom for the first meeting of the weekend. I got a little lost in the corridors on the way and was consequently one of the last to arrive. When I pushed open the thick wooden door, it revealed a high-ceilinged, opulent room absolutely full of disabled people. Momentarily, I froze in my tracks as a single thought echoed through my mind: 'Oh, God. I've got a disability.'

It was February 1993 and absolutely freezing in Darlington. The swim sessions were interspersed with meetings to discuss how the team might improve its training weekends, building on the performances of the Barcelona games, among other things. I'd enjoyed the weekend, but it had been a reality check in areas that I hadn't even thought there was reality to be checked. 'How can going to the Paralympics ever answer the dream of going to the Olympics?' I asked myself. 'Are the two the same? Are they equal?' I really didn't think they were.

Mentally, it was a retrograde step for me. My aspirations for swimming success were back in the gutter.

From this point I did the bare minimum to stay in the squad and hang out with my friends. During each training session I would do the necessary metres but my mind was unengaged. I would enter the occasional swimming competition to keep Mike happy, but I was losing interest in seeing how fast I could swim.

In spite of my apparent lack of enthusiasm, the ABS decided to pick me for a team they were sending to France in early April 1993. We arrived in the southern town of Perpignan. It was steeped in history, with the visual riches of the snow-capped Pyrenees rising spectacularly above its rooftops. The pool was an old one, though it had been well maintained. There were a few other European teams mixed in with French competitors who made up the bulk of the entry.

The event was far from slick. At the start of one of the early races a competitor dived in and his trunks fell down. It wasn't what I'd had in mind. If you made it to your block before your race started it was a minor miracle. It wasn't so much a language barrier as a cultural one. The organisers insisted on stopping the entire programme every few races in order that all the officials might have a cup of coffee or a small piece of cheese. I have never before or since seen a national stereotype played out in such accuracy.

My racing reflected my training – mediocre. But, as the new kid on the block, I was causing a bit of commotion. New competitors often just 'appear' in Paralympic sport as people have accidents or illnesses. Across a low-grade field I won the 100-metre butterfly and the 200-metre individual medley. It felt like a hollow victory. When we landed at Gatwick, both Mum and Dad were there to meet me and so thrilled upon seeing the two tinny gold medals as I tried to give a genuine smile.

Rule breaker

Just four weeks later I was sent with a slightly larger ABS team to a remote mining town called Skellefteå in northern Sweden. Although only 80 miles outside the Arctic Circle, it was surprisingly warm and the sky was so blue that I was constantly looking upwards. It ran much more smoothly than the meet in France, and all was going well until I got disqualified in the 100-metre butterfly, my main event. I had been swimming butterfly by breathing to my left side, the same side as my stroking arm. There is no rule in butterfly that says you have to breathe to the front, though there is one that states your shoulders must be even. Most able-bodied swimmers breathe to the front to make it easier to comply with this rule. The advantage of breathing to the side is that you can keep your body flatter and maintain a straighter and therefore shorter course.

But it didn't matter where I breathed – my shoulders were never going to be level. I was using the latitude of the international rulebook but still operating within its parameters. But the competition was under Swedish national rules, which were much more specific. The same rule saw me disqualified from the individual medley too. It would turn out to be a much larger problem than at first it seemed.

The experience of the two competitions did nothing to change my attitude towards swimming, the Paralympics or my disability. The whole thing was little more than a social gathering in my mind.

Wise words

After competing in my home pool, I was sitting upstairs in the café with my friends. It was a perfect teen hideout, full of games machines and noise, and just grimy enough to keep adults out. Which is why it was surprising when I saw a well-built man walking over to our table. He wasn't anyone I knew and I was surprised when he began talking to me. Without preliminaries, he said, 'I was really impressed with the swimming that you were doing in there.' He gestured to the window and down to the pool as I started going pink. 'You must be aiming for the Paralympics.'

I said, 'Nah, not really.'

'Oh, why's that?' His tone became almost accusatory.

'Well I'm just not that into it, er . . .'

He cut me off, having seen exactly where the conversation was going. 'Before you were ill you could do ten thousand things. Ten thousand. So now you can do nine thousand. Which means that you've got a choice: you can concentrate on the one thousand things that you can't do any more, or you can concentrate on the nine thousand things that you *can* still do.' He paused, his eyes burning as he had a fleeting look at each of the others before fixing back on me. His tone suddenly switched to one of almost timid politeness as he said, 'Anyway, just something to maybe think about.'

With that he gave a thin smile and walked out of the café, leaving me scarlet with embarrassment. I haven't seen him since and have always had to assume that he was a parent of a swimmer from another club. As I read it back now, it all sounds like something from Roald Dahl's *James and the Giant Peach*.

Sometimes Lady Luck will spark your Chimo Cycle. This guy was the right person, saying the right thing, at the right time. If in doubt refer back to Figure 3 in Chapter 1. It ignited something inside me. I looked at my friends sitting in the café and they didn't care that my arm was a little wonky, so why did I? Perhaps the guy was right.

That night I took out my Kingfisher *Children's Factfinder* and looked at the small paragraph about Mark Spitz for the first time in over two years. There was nothing to stop me if I decided to try to be the best I could be. So that was exactly what I decided to do.

My approach to training started to become much more precise. I was never going to be the tallest or strongest athlete, so I would have to concentrate on my strengths: good technique and mental toughness. I decided I would learn to think myself faster. I applied myself to doing everything that Mike set as correctly as possible. At first my mind just couldn't cope with the intensity of concentration: body position, hand position, breathing, kick and timing all had to be thought of simultaneously and all the time, and that was just basic technique. I set myself the small goal of changing something every training session, to try to learn how specifically to adjust individual parts of the stroke and how changing one part affected another. Some days, changing something meant stopping a part of the stroke changing, often under the pressure of fatigue. It became a source of ideas and inspiration for both Dad and me, and motivated us both.

At college I was coming unstuck. The first academic year was drawing to an end and I was starting to struggle more than my peers with the work. I was studying maths, physics and geography and, with the first two in particular, my knowledge carried over from school was full of holes. It was disheartening and started to fall into the shade of my enlightened outlook about swimming.

Learning curve

I was on a learning curve all the time with disability swimming, principally the way it worked and what you could say and what you couldn't. It surprised me the way that disabled people spoke to one another, talking frankly and often loosely about one another's impairment without batting an eyelid. About the only word that was off limits was 'handicapped'.

Provisionally, I had been given a domestic disability classification of S8. There are ten functional disability classifications with S1 being for those with most severe forms of impairment and S10, at the opposite end of the spectrum, for those with a minimal disability e.g. one hand or one foot missing. An S9 swimmer would be someone with a forearm missing or leg amputated above the knee and an S8 is a competitor without an entire arm or a condition affecting both legs. Since I couldn't use my arm I was in. In the summer of 1993 I became Short Course National champion (short-course racing is swum in a 25-metre pool; long-course is in a 50-metre Olympic-sized pool).

That National Championships was the first time I had ever seen a world record sheet. I had won the 100-metre butterfly in a time of 1:12.32, the world record for the more difficult long-course mark stood at 1:10.89 held by Erling Tromsden of Norway. When I saw who held the record I was surprised that I hadn't seen him earlier in the year in Sweden. One thing was for sure: on paper I had to find 1.43 seconds plus a little extra to compensate for the change of race format. I wanted that record.

August is the warmest month of the year in the UK and for some reason unknown to me the only month in which the swimming calendar shuts down. But early in September 1993 I got my first chance to race in a long-course competition in several years. Sheffield's mighty Pond's Forge complex, built for the 1991 World Student Games, had seen a hatful of able-bodied world records set in its crystal-clear water. I swam dreadfully. The two-week break I'd had in August had completely undermined my less than robust fitness. Every athlete needs a break to recharge themselves at the end of a tough season, but I hadn't had a tough season and I knew it. I got back into training and got my head down, concentrating on my strength of good technique.

The World Championships were the following year and, entering in 1994, I needed to have a good fitness base. I swam Club Championships at Braintree and got beaten by kids younger than I and hammered by my peers, but it didn't matter. I had a new course now. By early 1994 I planned to have a good aerobic base. The grinding weekend meets would have a purpose and hopefully my times would gradually start to fall.

World view

As time went by and I became more involved with disability sport, I gradually stopped seeing disabilities and started just seeing different shapes. I felt that I had crossed an evolutionary boundary in terms of my outlook. With that came the most surprising thing of all: more freedom. It dawned on me that I was completely free to subject a disabled person's personality to the same rigour I would anyone else's. More importantly, they would do the same with me.

As soon as it became obvious that I was still who I was and that lifting things down from high shelves was not the basis of whether one was a good person or not – except perhaps in a supermarket – I began to understand what it meant to be true to oneself. When that happened I effectively had my passport validated to visit whatever world I wanted, for as long as I wanted – be it royal, sporting, Paralympic, academic – and just be myself.

But 1993 had one last surprise. On Wednesday, 13 October, I got a glimpse of the world I was entering. One month prior, almost to the day, an official envelope arrived from the British Sports Association for the Disabled. Inside was an invitation printed on thick card with embossed blue lettering. It read, 'Her Royal Highness the Princess of Wales and the British Sports Association for the Disabled have the pleasure of inviting you to Grosvenor Square for a reception to celebrate the achievements of the British Team at the Barcelona 1992 Paralympics.' Perhaps they just didn't realise that I hadn't been part of the team, but I certainly wasn't going to argue.

At home it was a red-letter day, almost literally, given the postmark. My grandparents in particular were over the moon and Mum took me out to buy a suit. I prided myself in my ability to look scruffy all the time. When it came to formal wear, I was completely out of my depth and in the shop I had Mum, who made sure that the assistant knew precisely why we were buying it, and the shop assistant pulling jackets off the shelves with Olympian speed. I left with a blue blazer and trousers. The blazer was double-breasted with a little anchor on each button. It was also slightly too big. The overall effect was to make me look like an aspiring Captain Birdseye.

Dad drove me up to London, though unfortunately couldn't come in. We laughed together about how good it would have been if we could arrive in the Squanderbug. But, as I walked through the door, I didn't feel like me. People knew who I was without asking. Not as someone's son or someone ill. I was given a glass of champagne, made my way upstairs and was directed into a room with a large central table and opulent décor. A few swimmers were there but the bulk of the room was populated by powerful people of industry. We stood making polite chitchat.

At the point when I had exhausted all my conversation pertaining to polo, the master of ceremonies, dressed in a formal red uniform, announced, 'My lords, ladies and gentlemen, the Princess of Wales.' A large double door opened and there she was.

I don't know what I was expecting, perhaps that she would glow or have some sort of visible aura. This was the first famous person I had ever met, and possibly the most prominent woman in the world.

She looked incredibly stylish gliding around the room in a simple black dress. Two things struck me about her, that she seemed genuinely far more interested in the sportspeople in the room than anyone else and that she was funny. When she got to me I couldn't think of a single thing to say. She could see I was embarrassed and cracked a couple of jokes.

Hanging my blazer back in the wardrobe that night was surreal. I almost felt as if I should have left it at the reception.

With A levels coming into view, I was hopeful but not confident of getting into Leeds University, my first choice. I had an interview with Dr Andrew McCaig and explained the whole story. He weighed up my answers, occasionally chuckling through his goatee. My pot-holed education and meagre list of international swimming results reduced my entry requirements, though not by much.

The Commonwealth Games were due to be held in Victoria on the west coast of Canada that summer and for the first time ever at an able-bodied multi-sport event they were including disability events. There was one problem. The only event to be included was the S9 100-metre freestyle. England could send two male and two female swimmers. This would mean that I would have to beat swimmers who were less disabled than I was in an event in which I was not brilliant.

As the weeks went by, Mike angled my training programme to maximise my chances of qualifying. I tried to make every tumble-turn and every push-off as stream-lined as possible. At an April competition in the Dutch city of Deventer, I broke the world short-course record in the 100-metre butterfly. But a faster time was set by another S8 when Wayne Riding clocked a time of 1:07.66. It was out of reach and I knew it. No amount of positive thought was going to find me the best part of three seconds in three months. The other place had been secured by Phil Steadman, a much faster S9.

By May my final exams were in full swing – stressful and exhausting. I was devastated to have missed the Commonwealth team but swimming had to take a back seat until exams were over in June. I knew my results were in doubt.

As a consolation for missing out on Commonwealth qualification I was invited to go as part of a small team of eight to train at the British Olympic Association holding camp in Tallahassee in northern Florida. Climate-wise, it was a simulation camp for the Olympics in Atlanta in 1996.

The weather was hot and humid. Any item of clothing left outside for a short spell could cultivate enough amoebic life to start its own evolutionary chain. But this was exactly the point of the exercise. Just to stay functioning, we had to drink plenty of extra fluids and ensure that we were replacing lost salts.

The team was made up of six swimmers, one coach and a team manager. Four of the swimmers were male and I shared a room with Peter Hull, to this day one of the most inspirational people I have ever met. Pete has no legs and no forearms, and it was an education when he explained to me that he has an impairment – it's only his environment that makes him disabled. His most efficient way of swimming was on his back. With no large limbs to weigh him down he floated on the surface like a cork, propelling himself with his upper arms. Despite such limited functionality, he had incredible technique and was able to roll his body to the perfect angle to maintain a streamlined position yet allow his upper arm to bite in the water. As an S2, he was never going to super-quick, but it was easy to see why he was the best in the world at what he did.

Serious business

Patsy Coleman was the coach on the trip and had devised an individual programme for each of us. It was a punishing schedule, and, ten days into the three-week camp, cracks began to show, with little sign on the horizon of a break. I was stretching after a particularly hard set when one of the others said, 'I don't know why you bother doing that, I'm just treating this whole thing as a holiday.' I was incandescent and responded by telling her that she had no right to be wearing GB kit. Ultimately, I made it perfectly clear that I personally wanted nothing to do with her. The able-bodied athletes on the camp and the students at Florida State University were considerate but we were on trial for credibility and I didn't want someone else tarnishing my achievements. Later that night, she was in floods of tears and the next day I was in big trouble. I got a huge dressing down in front of the team, but later on Patsy said, 'You know I had to do that.'

On the final day of the camp we challenged the modern pentathletes (the five sports of the modern pentathlon being swimming, running, shooting, horse-riding and fencing) to a relay race whereby they would be bound by tape to match the disabilities we had. They were really up for it at first but started to lose enthusiasm when they saw just how little movement some of the team had. About halfway through, it started to become clear that we might have overdone the tape a little as one of the pentathletes started his length. He was simulating Pete's disability and had his wrists taped to his shoulders and his legs bound together at the ankle. He made it about two metres into the length and started to sink. Wondering at first whether he was putting it on, we let him lie on the floor of the pool for a while, but when he started to wriggle frantically about a couple of us jumped in to prop him up.

Back at home I went swimming at Braintree and felt incredible. I was slicing through the water. The Commonwealth Games started shortly afterwards. I was so envious watching the opening ceremony on TV. That emotion briefly evaporated when the Australian official, Arthur Tunstall, said the presence of athletes with a disability was 'an embarrassment to both sides . . . people have to go out of their way to assist them and able people are a little bit embarrassed to have them around'. The media hit the nail squarely on the head, branding the man an imbecile, and the games continued.

In mid-August, I got all the grades I needed bar one. It was a tense morning. I phoned the earth sciences department at Leeds University and nervously waited to speak to an admissions tutor. Mum sat with a hopeful look on her face as I was put on hold. A voice came on the other end and I explained my predicament. I was put back on hold. The voice came back on and said, 'That should be fine, Giles. We'll see you for the start of term in October.' Mum beamed at me.

When I got home I phoned the head coach at City of Leeds Swimming Club. I'd spoken to him once before to sound him out about joining the club. He was very positive, though this time there was the hint of a caveat in his tone. He explained that there were two top squads at the swimming club and I would be in a group called A2.

Joey Gardiner had also applied to Leeds, to read English. He sailed through his A-levels and got in without a hitch. We both applied to stay in the halls that claimed to have a 3:1 ratio of women to men, and both got rejected. But it turned out to be one of the best rejections of all time. Not only were we put in the same flat but on the very first day at Boddington student campus I met many of the friends that I still see frequently today.

As soon as I could, I drove my little blue Mini down to Leeds International Pool to start training with my new club, nervous and excited. The coach seemed like a nice guy and I saw a group of people who looked like serious swimmers getting ready to start training. We walked straight past them and to another group, in good shape but without the same focus. We'd walked past A1, and this was A2. Right from the outset it was obvious that you can give a group any name you want but there was clearly only one top squad, and A2 wasn't it. A1 had the toughest training regime, often fitting in nine or ten sessions a week, but they would do so under optimal conditions, getting the best schedule for their sessions in the best facilities available to the club. A2 would fit around them, often utilising inferior pools and sometimes training late at night. I couldn't help feeling that these conditions were by no means ideal for someone trying to make their way into elite competitions.

But at the time I thought perhaps I just had to prove myself to get into A1. With the World Championships in Malta in November, I had trained through the summer break and was still riding on the benefits of the training camp in Tallahassee. I hoped that, having proven my worth there, I would be in with a good chance of moving groups. What is it they say about assumption?

A class apart

The first month of university flew by and soon I was on the plane for the World Championships. Funding for disability swimming was tight, so there had been no formal trials for the competition. Instead, swimmers had to submit two official times from competitions between February and July. Checking in the team at the airport had taken an age, but it was worth it when we arrived on an idyllic, sun-drenched isle. Most of the teams were in the same massive hotel in an area that was far from safe.

There were five days before the week-long competition got under way, not long enough to properly acclimatise. But all of the teams were operating on a shoestring and, like us, had arrived just a few days before the start of the event. Two days before the opening ceremony, I was summoned to my international classification test. Thankfully, I didn't realise the significance of the test, or else I would have been a nervous wreck.

Until that point I'd had a domestic classification but if I was going to compete internationally I would have to go through a much more rigorous version of the test conducted by a group of foreign classifiers.

There were five of them. Two from Brazil, one each from Spain, Iceland and Japan. None spoke English. Through a waving of hands I was able to understand what they wanted me to do. I swam each stroke several times to a distance of about 15 metres and back with all of them peering and pointing at various parts of my stroke. After that it was onto the side for a physiotherapist to carry out the 'dry' part of the test. He was assessing movement to see if I was faking or not. Careers are made and broken in the classification test: move up and it could mean your career is over before you've even started; move down and you will be strongly competing against more disabled athletes.

There was a lot of discussion for five people who between them spoke four different languages. I got dressed and sat waiting to hear the outcome. Finally, I heard I was an eight.

The first International Paralympic Committee (IPC) World Swimming Championships opened with a Maltese military band playing and marching around the poolside. Balloons ended up in the pool prematurely and the fireworks seemed pointless, as it was still daylight. As the wind shifted, the Great Britain team, sitting level with the start line, got showered with ash. The next day was the first of the programme and the S8 200-metre individual medley (IM) would be my first event. My main event, the 100-metre butterfly, fell on Day Two.

I got up early, had a light breakfast and made my way to the pool. It was an outdoor pool with a sizable spectator stand up one side. I got changed and started my warm-up, all the time looking out for the competition. I had seen the start sheet and not recognised a single name.

Warm-up felt good and sharp. I got dressed and waited quietly for my heat to be called. The first time in the call-up room is always a little scary – I was very aware that if I was late I might miss the race, but if I was too early I would be penned into a small space for too long. The room was almost full when I arrived and I immediately started putting faces to names. Erling Tromsden looked nothing like I imagined. He was a very serious-looking man with a face of iron and a moustache like that of Mark Spitz. I looked for his disability and saw that both of his legs were amputated at the knee. He looked at me and knew exactly who I was.

I laboured in the 200-metre IM heat and felt that I just couldn't get going. It was a surprise to see that, after both heats had finished, I was the fastest qualifier, bemusing but promising. I swam in the diving pit for 1,200 metres to disperse the lactic acid in my bloodstream, got dressed and headed back to the hotel.

It was a starry evening as I walked out under the floodlights for the final. It was chilly but, with adrenalin coursing through my veins, I didn't feel a thing.

I felt ready to go physically but mentally I was nowhere and everywhere. I had come here to win the 100-metre butterfly, but here I was in Lane 4, the fastest qualifier for the 200-metre IM with a world-class field either side of me. Over the next three minutes I was taught a serious lesson. When I looked at the start sheet after the race properly I noticed a step in the entry times. The first seven were all fairly evenly matched, as were the next nine but with a gap of about three seconds separating swimmers 7 and 8.

The race went out on the butterfly leg at a blistering pace. This was my strongest stroke, yet at the first 50-metre mark I was only a metre in front. I saw everyone sail past me on backstroke. I managed to claw back to third on the breaststroke leg but lost ground again on the freestyle. I finished sixth, a long way behind the winner, Jean-Jacques Terblanche of South Africa, who had set a new world record in the lane next to me. As I swam down I gave myself a hard time for not having my mind properly on the job.

The following day started exactly the same, except that I knew what I was doing, as I had dwelled on this day for several months. I cruised through Heat 3 and qualified fastest for the final. This time there was going to be no messing about with pace, as I checked down the time sheet to see that everyone was pretty much on their entry time. I watch Tromsden swim his heat and was impressed by his technique. For a man with no feet he managed to get fantastic propulsion from his undulation. But his time was up and mine was about to begin and, with that, I returned to the hotel to rest.

Stroke setback

I sat on the front seat of the bus smiling to myself, but every British team member who got on gave me a sympathetic look. As I chatted to the coach sitting next to me I heard I'd been disqualified for a dropped shoulder. Exactly the same as in Sweden in 1993. My blood ran cold. Was this the end of my swimming career before it had even started?

At the hotel I was met on the steps by Patsy Colemen, who was holding a fresh bag of kit and a packed lunch. We got in a taxi and went back to the pool. By now the sun was high in the sky and, although it was November, it was beating down. That was the first time I had met Anne Green, head of IPC Swimming. She was a no-nonsense Aussie who said what she wanted, when she wanted. And she said things I didn't want to hear.

It transpired that the Norwegian team, seconded by the Swedish team, had put in a protest about my technique. Swimming butterfly with one arm and breathing to the side was too much like freestyle. Perhaps they had a point, but I could not believe that this problem had never come up before.

The sticking point was my uneven shoulders and the able-bodied rule book said they had to be level. But there wasn't a single one-armed swimmer who could ever keep their shoulders even on any stroke, let alone butterfly, whichever way they breathed. Our tack was that, if they didn't allow me to swim, they would have to remove all other swimmers who were swimming in a more conventional style.

The conversation became more heated as I stayed out in the sun, swimming demonstration lengths for classifiers, for over three hours. Patsy was doing a great job of arguing my case. Their case for disqualification finally collapsed when she pointed out that the previous day I had swum the 200-metre individual medley, which contains butterfly. If they were going to disqualify me for the butterfly but not the medley, they were admitting incompetence. Bingo! I was back in. But Anne Green made it perfectly clear that after this competition they would revise the rules and require all S8 swimmers to breathe either to the front or to the opposite side of their stroking arm on butterfly.

I got back to the hotel and had just enough time to get my kit together to head back, aware that all my competitors would have spent the day resting before the final. In the warm-up I felt slick and was having so much fun I didn't want to get out of the pool. I felt alert, awake and completely relaxed. I sat in the stand cheering on my teammates and enjoying the occasion. I knew what I had to do when my name was called and I walked down to the call-up room and checked in. A problem with the printer that day had meant that the list of finalists had gone up very late. Tromsden was already in there and clearly surprised to see me. 'I bet you are, mate,' I thought. He wandered over on his prosthetic legs and said 'So you have to change your technique?'

'Nope,' I responded to his stern yet puzzled face. I wasn't going to give him an inch. As I walked away I got a surge of adrenalin that I'd never felt before. I stood in the corner trying to shut out all the commotion of the call-up room.

As we walked out to the start I got a massive cheer from the team and supporters. I'd gone from overdog, to nowhere-dog, to underdog all in a day and it had got people fired up. Although I had qualified fastest, the first three were separated by just under one second and we had all swum in separate heats.

The movements of my fingers felt incredibly swift and precise as I suckered goggles into my eye sockets. Three short whistles sounded before a fourth, longer, whistle called me to my block. I stood motionless on top with my heart rate firm and fast but not racing. 'Take your marks!' I moved to the front of the block, clasping the front lip with my left hand. As the first quivering waves of the start signal hit my ears, I moved.

I hit the water and began kicking to the surface. With each kick I was surging forward with complete ease and when I broke the surface my stroke ran like clockwork. In Lane 5 and outward all I could see was bit of light splash as I reached the 25-metre mark, but

Tromsden was in Lane 3 on my right and he was where the danger lay. I neared the turn. The floodlights above the water did little to illuminate the wall under its surface, so I could barely see the line on the bottom. It would be difficult to get the turn right. I got to where I thought the wall was and stretched my arm forward. My hand connected perfectly with the timing pad as if it were part of my stroke. As I turned I flashed a look across the pool. There was no one there – either a really good or really bad sign.

The lactic acid started to burn 20 metres from the end of the race, but I pushed ever harder, aware that the gloomy light may have concealed my rivals. I hit the wall and gasped for breath. I read the scoreboard three times, making sure that it was my name that had '1:08.77, 1st' next to it. I could not believe what it said. Tromsden had come second and, like me, had also broken the world record.

I felt incredible. I was marshalled away for the medal ceremony, completely blown away by the massive improvement in my personal best. For the first time I received a medal while watching the raising of the Union Flag with the GB team members singing the national anthem at the tops of their lungs. That night I was completely shattered but didn't sleep a wink. I kept thinking of the time. With the change of rules it was a world record that would stand for six years.

For the rest of the competition I was part of the ever-growing number of swimmers whose principal job it was to cheer on teammates. The sun made way for torrential rain over much of the rest of the week. Although the medals kept rolling in, it set the tone for our arrival back home.

Upon arrival at the airport we were all bussed to a nearby hotel to meet media and give interviews. We expected the place to be packed. But, the night before, it transpired that Bruce Grobbelaar, the Liverpool goalkeeper, had been accused by the *Sun* of throwing matches. Only five reporters showed up. It was a dampener on a highly successful and fun-filled trip.

Dad collected me from the hotel. When we reached the car we both opened a door and I said, 'I guess that makes me world champion.'

He said, 'I guess it does.'

We grinned at each other and drove home.

Chapter Six

Troughs and Peaks

Reaction at university was muted, and understandably so. Here was a guy most people had known for just a month, who then disappeared for three weeks and came back proclaiming to be world champion, without so much as molecule of print ink to confirm it. It didn't bother me, why would they know?

But it did bother me when I went to training at City of Leeds. Despite having told the club that I was heading for the World Championships at the time, this fact seemed to have been forgotten and people were more likely to ask where I'd been than how the competition had gone. That really hurt, and I realised for the first time how important it was for me also to feel part of a team.

And the assumption I had made about proving myself to get into A1 was so misguided as to be naïve. Even as world champion and record holder, I still wasn't given the chance to change squads.

Technical hitch

I was struggling to rebuild my stroke after the rule change, too. Trevor was a lovely man, and gave up a lot of his time for the swimming club, but his approach was to focus on strength and raw fitness through metre upon metre in the pool. Every time I tried to lift my head forward, my feet dropped to the floor. Without the additional momentum of my right arm going forward, I was swimming with a rocking motion rather than a dolphin motion. It was so inefficient that I struggled to complete 50 metres and hold form.

The bright lights of university life glowed brilliantly as I made more friends. In contrast, the lack of progress I was making at the swimming club was draining my motivation by the day, and it quickly became a vicious circle. The longer I stayed in A2, the more my motivation dropped, the less I was inspired by the whole sport and the less I went training. There was less than two years to the Paralympics in Atlanta and I had a chance of winning the 100-metre butterfly but I felt I was banging my head against a brick wall.

Instead of getting frustrated, I should have turned my attention to creating much smaller Chimo Cycles. Smaller changes rather than large and slices instead of slabs of inspiration would still have gone on to yield motivation.

The first set of university exams came in late January. There were European Championships that year and they were due to be held in Perpignan, in the pool where I had swum my first international. Mentally I was burnt out. Cancer, exams, then the highs of the World Championships and the pitfalls of Leeds Swimming Club had left me drained. Exams were looming once more at university. I could not be bothered even to try, knowing the results would not have an input into my final degree grade. I failed four out of six.

It was time to decide what I wanted. To engage in trying to motivate myself, to set my sights lower or set them on something else – any one of the above would produce the change needed to keep the Chimo Cycle turning.

Initially, it didn't hit home quite how serious it was. I pressed on with university and swimming, training properly some weeks but not others. I could almost hear people saying, 'Well, of course, a *real* Olympian would be so single-minded that they'd just get themselves to the pool no matter what'.

Maybe they would.

Stagnation

The temperature was soaring and it was set to be the hottest year since the famous drought of 1976. I loved university but resented the choice I had to make between sport and education every time I went training. I was supposed to be mastering a new style of butterfly so that I could build on my success at the World Championships and move forward towards my dream of Paralympic gold. But I hadn't changed a thing in weeks. My swimming had stagnated.

People headed back to the four corners of the country for the Easter holidays. For me it was a four-week window to get in some decent training at Braintree. It was a breath of fresh air to see friendly faces and swim in an open environment. The first thing I did was a session on my own with Dad and Mike trying to figure out the best way to adjust my stroke to fit the rules. Mike kept saying that if I was an able-bodied swimmer we'd just take a textbook off the shelf and read about it. But we had to create something entirely new. The best we could do was to apply the knowledge that we had between the three of us to try things out.

We tried everything we could think of, timed every single variation and measured heart rates as accurately as we could, searching for the variation with the highest efficiency. It soon became obvious that breathing to the right and stroking with the left was the fastest way of doing it. That way I could keep my body as flat as possible, and that had two major advantages: first, my legs didn't want to sink; and, second, it kept my shoulders as flat as possible. However, putting my left hand in one direction while turning my head to the other was difficult to do on dry land, let alone in the water. It also meant that my head could begin to turn only once my hand was clear of the water and had to be centred again before my hand entered the water. Consequently my mouth was out of the water for a much shorter period of time, leaving much less time to breathe. If I was going to learn to do it at all, I would not only have to master a complete retiming of the stroke cycle but would also have to do it with less air.

As I practised this new style of butterfly, new problems began to emerge. The stroke was so flat that, as fatigue set in, my left hand would start to skip across the surface of the water, which was illegal. The shortening of the breathing cycle meant having to draw air in as quickly as I possibly could, and with my mouth so close to the waterline this style of swimming was particularly prone to breathing in water and choking.

With the basics of a new stroke in place, I had a foundation on which I could build. I sat down with Mike and explained the problems I was having at the swimming club in Leeds. Together we came up with a plan: a series of way-marker target times that I had to hit at specific points throughout the calendar leading all the way through the European Championships, the Paralympic Trials and the games itself. Linked in to the target times was a progression of stroke changes that we thought I needed to master at each point, and I would go back home at least once a month for him and Dad to make sure that I was getting it right. On top of the whole series of changes to keep me engaged in working towards the Paralympics, Mike drew up a week-by-week list of main training areas that I needed to hit.

Chimo in action

I couldn't wait to start university after the break and was excited about swimming, too. From then on, I was a member of the swimming club on paper but resigned myself to using it as a facility for lane training, nothing more. It was still far from perfect. But I was determined to find the positives in the situation; after all, it was my decision to stay. One major plus is that I got to train in a 50-metre pool and was therefore swimming double the distance each length before getting the micro-rest that a swimmer gets each turn. Breathing to the opposite side of stroking was putting an enormous load across my left shoulder, as it not only had to power my left arm but also support the twisting force of lifting the majority of my torso out of the water.

Leeds International Pool was a peculiar design. The four walls of the building and the pool inside were offset by 45 degrees so that the pool appeared to be set diamond-shaped within the building. This produced weird triangular spectator stands whereby the back row was a lone seat in the centre. It was also one of the few pools in the country to have a 10-metre diving platform. But, instead of having a separate diving pit, it merely joined onto the side of the main pool about halfway along. This meant that, if you were swimming in Lane 1, you would have the wall down one side of the lane until you were just past a third of the length, when it would fall away to a deep-blue depth of 5 metres.

I would often train in Lane 1 and used the diving pit's start and finish as way markers for developing my new butterfly. It was too far at first just to swim the new style all the time, so I broke it up into chunks. At first I would say to myself, 'I'll swim as perfectly as possible until I get to the start of the diving pool.' At this point I would put in a few strokes, breathing to my left side, and then try to carry on the rest of the length breathing to my right. When I had mastered that I would aim for where the diving pit rejoined the pool, then for a complete length, then for a length with a perfect turn, and so on until I could do a full one hundred. If my hand skipped the surface, I swallowed water or had to breathe to the left, that length wouldn't count. In my head I kept a tally of all the lengths I had completed within the rules against the total and gave myself a percentage score at the end of each training session.

I was using small Chimo Cycles as the foundation for a larger one (see Figure 2 in Chapter 1).

Mostly, I moved in the right direction with the

percentage of lengths done correctly going up, but often there were days when my shoulder was so tired I thought it was going to fall off. I had found a new motivation in mentally locking myself away, but I couldn't help feeling envious to the core when I saw A1 walk onto poolside. I went to the gym with them a couple of times. The other swimmers were friendly but all had things they should be doing and went about it systematically – having taken myself out of the squad system, I no longer had a team to be a part of.

Sport versus education

The failed exam modules from the end of the first semester were coming back to haunt me. I needed them to move on to the second year and so had to pass the resits. If the exams weren't a problem, the dates of them were. They clashed almost to the day with the European Championships in early August 1995. I was in trouble. The worst-case scenario could mean severely denting my swimming hopes or being thrown out of university. My personal tutor made it perfectly clear that it was university or swimming. As he said it my blood ran cold. But then I thought, 'Am I giving up too easily here?' So I went to see the head of department.

Joe Cann had seen things almost beyond the imagination, having visited the floor of the Atlantic Ocean in a submersible. There he was one of the first people to witness hydrothermal vents called black smokers, which spew out thousands of gallons of superheated water at 300 degrees Celsius, laden with toxic metals. The lightless existence of the ecosystems that lived around the vents had given scientists new directions in thinking about the origins of life on Earth. He had also been part of the team that developed the theory of plate tectonics, explaining how the Earth's crust moves and why mountains, volcanoes and earthquakes occur where they do.

When I explained my predicament to him he rocked back in his chair, his fingertips touching like a pitched rooftop. I sat awaiting his judgement. When he spoke it was soft yet measured. 'You have been very careless, Giles, very careless indeed. In my experience, people in your situation often don't stay the course.' Then he grinned. 'But yours is a special case. If I can fix this for you I don't want to see you in here again asking for the same thing. Is that clear?' I nodded so positively my head was in danger of falling off. 'All right then, we'll reschedule your re-examination for when you come back. Do not fail this time.'

With that we shook hands and I walked to the door. Just as I opened it he said, 'Giles, will I be able to place a bet on this, er, European Championships?' I didn't fail a single exam or test in the rest of my time at university.

I was making good progress with the new technique and qualified for the European championship, team but there was one part of the 'new butterfly' I was really struggling with. As I got more tired throughout the race I found it harder to get my head back to the centre, as I needed ever more oxygen to fuel a fatigued left shoulder and stop my hand trailing in the water. I was taking too long over the breathing cycle to draw in air but, with the championships approaching, I was running out of time to correct the fault. I was now inside the rules but the whole thing felt stop/start, as if I was in charge of a collection of gifted individuals who found it impossible to work together as a team.

With term finished I headed back to Braintree to work with Mike in the run-up to the championships. The final few weeks are the most crucial. This period is called the taper, and during the last twenty-one days my programme moved away from aerobic fitness to sprints and speed-sharpening work. In this period it is not possible to make yourself swim any faster on race day, but get it wrong and you will swim a whole lot slower.

We landed at Perpignan with just two days to go before the competition's launch. There was no opening ceremony this time, just a local singer pushing out the French national anthem, and then it was straight down to business. The programme was a carbon copy of the World Championships nine months before, so my 200-metre individual medley was on the first day and my

100-metre butterfly on the second of a seven-day competition.

Energy quest

After Day 1, I had a European bronze medal to my name. It was a great boost going into the butterfly the following day, but I was concerned. There hadn't been so much as a murmur from the officials and I had managed to do the first length in exactly the same time as if I had been breathing to the left. The problem lay in the amount of energy the first 50 metres had burned up. I was able to maintain the speed but it was leaving a lot less stamina for the remainder of the race. I had seen Tromsden in training and his stroke looked smooth and effortless.

I was up early the next day, eager to make sure my body was fully awake and ready. I was sharing with Peter Hull and we had both shaved down the night before and there was hair everywhere in the bathroom. So much so that I slipped on the tiles while brushing my teeth and nearly didn't make it to the pool at all.

It was the second time I had ever shaved off all my body hair for a swimming competition, but there was something about the water in the Perpignan pool that made it feel like the first. When I first hit the water I felt like a knife separating two pieces of paper. Conscious all the time that I needed to be fast but not extravagant with energy consumption, I was as smooth as possible, letting the chain of power pass unhindered from my arm stroke to my leg kick and back again. It still felt like a collection of motions attached to a body rather than a single body of motion. But it was all I had and I sailed through the heats.

At a European level the depth in the S8 100-metre butterfly was not as frightening as at world level and I was convinced that it would come down to Tromsden and myself for the number-one spot. He too had cruised through the heats and, to my disappointment, did not seem surprised by my new technique – perhaps because he could see that it wasn't functioning quite right and my heat time at 1:11.04 was considerably slower than my own world record, as well as being slower than his best. This time I went back to the hotel to rest before the final.

For those few hours I tried not to sleep for fear of feeling drowsy before the event. Instead, I lay on my bed reading, listening to music and thinking about how I was going to swim the race in the afternoon. I couldn't change my technique, strength or level of fitness. All I could do was focus on the pacing. If I was going to be in with a chance, I would have to turn level with Tromsden. The trick would be to do it with enough juice in the tank for the way home. I was going to have to be swimming at maximum speed but not maximum energy consumption.

How you can be at top speed but at the same time

not consuming energy at a maximum rate? At the time I had a blue Mini that had an engine of 1000cc. It was a superb little car but because of its tiny engine size it would not accelerate going up steep hills. Even if I pushed the accelerator to the floor or kept it depressed to around three-quarters, the speed wouldn't change. But if I had my foot to the floor it would burn a lot more petrol. If I was in that car going up the hill I had to resist the temptation to press my foot to the floor.

World champion

I felt good in the warm-up and waited for my race wrestling with nervous flutters. It rankled with me that I had won at world level but there were people who didn't recognise the victory in the light of the rule changes. This was my chance to prove that they could do whatever they wanted I would still come out on top.

In the call-up room I didn't speak to anyone. Not even the marshals, just a nod to confirm my name. The eight of us sat in a line with the S9 butterfly swimmers getting ready behind us. I sat silent.

After twenty minutes we made our way out to the pool. The GB team were at the start end and as always making a lot of noise. I had qualified fastest which, had supplied me with Lane 4. Tromsden, just one-tenth of a second slower, was in five. Tromsden was on my left and I would yet again have to wait until the halfway point before I knew where he was.

The pool fell silent as the starter raised a hand. Within a handful of seconds we were off. I didn't notice the icy water, all the time thinking, 'Don't panic, don't panic!' I tried to stay fast but smooth. At 40 metres I had to draw in more air than normal. At 45 metres my hand skipped the water twice. Then the turn. Out of the corner of my left eye I could see we were level. I was still in it and it gave me a boost. The turn allowed a brief micro-rest from stroking. I was up on the surface again at 6 metres.

I could now see Tromsden every time I breathed and was shocked that I hadn't taken more ground off him around the turn. We were level coming down the second fifty and my shoulder was starting to burn. In the final 20 metres I moved in front and fought to the finish with my technique disintegrating with every stroke. I finished in a time of 1:10.81. The new rules had cost me over two seconds but I was still under Tromsden's previous world record. As we waited for the referee to signal us to clear the pool he shook my hand, gave me a big smile and hearty congratulations. We never raced again.

A stomach bug put me out of the freestyle relay, but in that competition I also won a silver medal as part of the 4 x 100 medley relay. I had been so wrapped up in my individual swims that they had both come and gone in a flash.

Back at home I sorted my resits and had a week off, waiting for September when training and the Paralympic season would start. I was world and European champion. I had successfully hit every stepping stone on the way to being able to hold the sparkling lustre of a gold medal and call it my own. All I had to do was prove myself again.

I was well and truly locked into a strong Chimo Cycle.

With Dad and Mike watching over every technical change and coming up with new ideas, we carried on constructing a new way of swimming, taking what we could from able-bodied coaching knowledge and moulding it to fit the unbalanced single-arm stroke. Even though I was implementing changes as fast as I could, I was falling behind the targets we'd set. Still, the problem was centring my head. If it was not exactly centred by the time my hand entered the water the whole stroke would unravel. My hand would wander across the centre line, causing the first part of the pull to be wasted or, if I was really tired, pull me off course. With that we decided to draw up a plan of smaller incremental changes to prevent me from losing heart.

The first year of university had been spent in college accommodation. The second year was in a house on Ash Road close to Headingley cricket ground. Seven of us moved into a house designed for four that had been carved up to create extra bedrooms. While looking round for new accommodation, we had come across every type of landlord imaginable. Most were pushy and tried to get a contract signed on the spot. One even showed us a house with only three beds. When we looked at him perplexed he said in all seriousness that if we had two per bed and one in the lounge we'd be fine.

Own slant

It was business as usual at the swimming club and I carried on putting my own slant on the sessions I was set. With each session my butterfly got smoother as I began to learn the new timing of the stroke, implementing one new change per week. That November I had my most successful Short Course Nationals ever, winning seven events. It reminded me of the Mark Spitz paragraph I had read many years before in *Children's Factfinder*.

My bedroom was on the top floor of the house and three mornings each week I would tiptoe down the stairs at a quarter past five to go training. The only problem arose from my clumsiness, which often resulted in my making a racket. Training in the early hours of the morning in winter has and will always be the toughest part of the sport. The big swimming competitions are in the summer, leaving the winter months to grind out metre after metre in the pool, and the able-bodied meets that I could hit the entry times for were far from glamorous. Early mornings, when it was quite possible to do a training session and get back home before it got light, and evening training sessions that got in the way of socialising all brought familiar calls from people talking of sacrifice. But I still didn't see it that way. It was a choice, my choice, and nothing more.

My degree work had continued to get incrementally more difficult, almost mirroring the increased work rate in the pool. I knew that a mistake academically now would cost me dearly and I had learned my lesson.

Paralympic Trials

Medically I was fine, except that my prosthesis had started to dislocate. The temporary top half of my prosthesis had a very small ball at its end, and it had worked itself free of the joint. Each time I lifted my right arm up from the elbow, the top of the prosthesis tried to push itself through the skin. As a defence my body had formed a fluid ball the size of a ping-pong ball that protruded forward from the shoulder. It looked very unsightly. With an additional 200 miles, the trip to see Mr Cannon took longer than it had ever done before. True to form, he wanted to get to work straightaway, having suspected that a final operation to introduce a new, more rounded head to the prosthesis would be needed. 'Is there any chance we could just hold off until late August?' I said.

With a smile he held his chin and said, 'My diary is that of a busy man Mr Long. But I suppose we could just about hold off until after the Paralympic Games.'

Paralympic Trials were in May at Pond's Forge, the finest swimming pool in the country. Every time I walk into the building I think it's fantastic. Its crystal-clear blue water is covered with a curved roof of latticed silver tubes. There is something about its architecture that says 'Sheffield', heavy and industrial yet at the same time with a tone of precision and quality. With all the lights turned on it was so dazzlingly bright that I had to use my outdoor mirrored goggles. Concerned it would be a sell-out, my parents had already bought the flights and tickets to not only my events but the opening ceremony too. Not qualifying was not an option.

Soon I headed back to Braintree to work with Mike on the final eight weeks before flying out to the holding camp in Pensacola, Florida. Mike also worked for Braintree Council and was able to access better pool times. We made the morning sessions slightly later and brought the evening sessions forward by an hour. This made my training times exactly the same time as heats and finals in Atlanta. I had also managed to pick up lost ground and was back on track with the original target times and stroke changes we had agreed.

Each time I went to the pool in Braintree, people I didn't know would wish me luck. Each time it happened it served as a small reminder of how close it was getting. There were no more technical changes to make at this late stage and I really believed the stroke was near perfect. Each session, Mike and I would work on making my technique faster, sharper, crisper, cleaner and more economical. I was using a series of Chimo Cycles inside one another that were motivating me on many levels. So, even though with three weeks to go I felt as if it were never going to end, I still had bulletproof motivation. The closer the calendar moved to the games, the further away it seemed to be. With six months to go it had felt as if there were no time to do anything; now there was only two weeks, it stretched out like a seven-year-old's summer holiday.

Atlanta

Ten days before I was due to fly out with the team, the Atlanta 1996 Olympic Games opened. It was the centenary games and many had said that it should have gone back to Athens. But few nations can do glitz like the Americans and the opening ceremony was spectacular. As the British team walked into the stadium I felt a quivering nervous excitement I'd never experienced before. The stadium erupted when special guest Muhammad Ali arrived. They presented him with a replica of his Olympic gold won at the 1960 games in Rome. He had tossed the original medal into the Ohio River after being refused service at a 'whites-only' restaurant.

Swimming ran the first week, with track and field

the second. I studied the coverage avidly, trying to envisage what it would be like when I was there. Every swimming race had me on the edge of my seat. The Russian Alexander Popov became the first man successfully to defend the 100-metre freestyle since Johnny Weissmuller (a.k.a. the movie world's Tarzan) in the 1920s. Great Britain was struggling until Paul Palmer won silver in the 400-metre freestyle and was then followed by Graeme Smith, who won a bronze in the 1,500-metre freestyle.

But the swimmer whom everyone was talking about was the Irish Michelle Smith (now Michelle de Bruin). She had seemingly come from nowhere to win three gold medals. The Americans were crying foul and most dismissed their claims, but they were right. Two years later she broke Irish hearts when she was banned for four years after tampering with a urine test.

The news was dominated by stories of corruption within the organising committee, of bribes paid to International Olympic Committee members and of a transport system that couldn't get anyone anywhere. A frustrated Steve Redgrave and Matthew Pinsent were forced to commandeer a bus to get them to Lake Lanier. There were reports that the games were 'too commercialised'. Then, on 27 July, a bomb went off in Centennial Olympic Park, killing two and injuring many more. For Great Britain the games were nothing short of a disaster, as the team finished thirty-sixth on the overall medals table, the nation's worst result ever. To round off, Juan Antonio Samaranch, the president of the IOC, broke with tradition by failing to hail Atlanta as the best Olympics ever, a telling omission.

So, while every games that I had ever seen had been packed with superlatives, these, in which I was taking part, were going to be rubbish. I tried to switch off to adverse comments.

Arriving at the airport was the first time I got a sense of the scale of the team. Arrayed before me were hundreds of athletes and well-wishers, with numerous bags of luggage and technical equipment. There was a short transfer upon arrival to the holding camp at a military base in Pensacola, on the coast in northern Florida.

The two weeks leading into the games were: swim, eat, sleep, rest and drink. Then drink some more. The climate was the same as Atlanta's, none of us liked it. Many of the athletes hadn't experienced close heat like it before and were struggling to consume enough fluid. For the lucky few the trip to Tallahassee two years before was really proving its worth.

Mind games

I knew I had qualified as fastest in the world. Yet every day I would spend two ten-minute periods rehearsing the 100-metre butterfly in my head. I had been doing it for weeks beforehand, but in the US it became much easier to envisage. I tried to cover everything: the colour of the pool, the temperature of the water and what it felt like, the size of the crowd, the noise, the light level, the scoreboard, the surface of the blocks, every lane, the height of the block above the water, the sound of the starting gun, the adrenalin rush, the rotation of the turn, the agony down the second length and hitting the wall at full extension. I never allowed myself to think about getting a medal. Before I had left, Mike had given me a full set of sessions and said, 'Remember to think about process, not outcome. Thinking about receiving a gold medal won't get you one.'

Four days before the games were due to start, the team took a four-hour bus journey up to Atlanta. As we drove into the city all we saw was one bill board for the Paralympics. Eventually we got to the athletes' village and waited to get our accreditation. Several large teams had arrived at the same time and there seemed to be a queue for everything, none longer than that for the food hall. Fortunately, I had my roommate Chris Holmes on hand to pass the time.

Chris is one of the greatest Paralympians of all time. Atlanta was his third Paralympics and great things were expected of him. He had won a staggering nine gold medals in Barcelona. At the Europeans the previous year we got on famously and decided to be roommates at the Games. Chris has a condition called retinal detachment, though few cases are as acute as his. On 20 June 1986, aged fourteen, he went to bed and woke up the next morning unable to see. He went blind literally overnight. Still, not only was he highly intelligent, having studied at Cambridge, but was also unbelievably funny.

When we eventually made it to our room it wasn't how I had pictured the Paralympics would be. The sheets on the bed were dirty and there was vomit on the floor. In the kitchen area there was evidence that a small fire had taken place and the microwave door was screwed shut. Worse was to come.

The GB team were all in a section of the village near the perimeter fence. As the Paralympics has fewer competitors than the Olympics, less space is needed within the village. The edge of the Paralympic village was inside that of the Olympic village, leaving a row of empty buildings just outside our bedroom window. The Olympic organising committee and the Paralympic organising committee had been at loggerheads for months. The land, owned by the Olympic organisers, had been sold. Rather than wait for the Paralympics to finish, a crane with a wrecking ball moved in and began knocking it down yards from the window on our second day there.

Class act

With just one day to go until the opening ceremony there was another shock. I had been under the misapprehension that once an athlete had an international classification they were bound to that class. In order to make sure that the system was as rigorous as possible the International Paralympic Committee carries out random reclassifications. The vast majority of the time nothing happens, and the athlete remains in the class into which they were originally assigned. Not this time. Just three days before the 100-metre butterfly a Danish swimmer named Emil Brondum moved down from an S9 to an S8. His main event was the 100-metre butterfly and on paper he was half a second quicker than I was. I heard this from a teammate while walking back from Georgia Tech. I managed to stay calm on the outside. All along, despite all the training, competing, rule changes and discrimination, there had been a voice inside me asking, 'Is this too easy?' It wasn't now.

The opening ceremony was awesome. The main stadium was at capacity and, with 110,000 people in their seats, we were outside waiting for the celebration to begin. As the sun began to set, the noise seemed to die away. It was possible to make out a bald-headed eagle soaring high above the stadium. It flew around the stands three times before landing on the glove of a falconer. Upon seeing this symbol of national pride the American audience went stratospheric. That's when the teams began filing in.

Opening ceremony

The teams were announced in alphabetical order, and we waited as it moved towards Great Britain. We watched Germany walk out to a warm reception. Then it was our turn. Everyone in the team was stamping their feet, shouting and cheering. I felt about half my weight. With the team emerging from the tunnel we were announced; the noise was beyond anything I had ever experienced. As we made our way around the track I could see Union Flags everywhere, and even managed to spot my family all frantically waving with big, beaming smiles.

After one complete circuit we were ushered to our seats in the centre of the stadium. I had almost stopped noticing that other teams were still coming in – until, last of all, they announced the host nation. The announcer barely managed to get the letter 'U' of 'United' out before the stadium erupted. With that, Aretha Franklin took to the stage and started belting out soul classics one after the other. As she hit the final few bars of 'Respect', a firework display started with an intensity that I have never seen since. There was not a square inch of black in the night sky. I was buzzing when I returned to the village. Many of the athletes who had been to Paralympic Games before had decided not to go to save their energy. Chris spent a few hours scraping me off the ceiling.

The next day we were into it, the first day of competition. The GB team had been allocated team space at the far end of the pool at the turn end. As we approached the towering Georgia Tech pool in silence, I began to get in the right frame of mind for the 200-metre IM. It wasn't easy. With the advent of Brondum, I had been in damage-limitation mode, entirely focused on the butterfly.

Warm-up felt OK but not spectacular. Everything seemed to be as good as I could make it but my body position felt low in the water. It was having a slight knock-on effect with the timing across all four strokes. My sprint times were spot on but I felt I had used too much energy to achieve them.

The heat swim was hard work and coming down the final 50 metres I felt as if I might not have anything more for the final. I had qualified for the final fifth fastest. Quickest was Terblanche of South Africa who had broken the world record. A medal in this race would be a tough call. I made my way back to my room and waited for the final.

In the evening warm-up I felt considerably better but still slightly off the boil. I spent longer than normal in the water as a way of keeping my nerves under control. It worked, but didn't produce any sharpening of technique.

With my full Great Britain Paralympic tracksuit on I made my way to the call-up room. It was difficult to stay calm. I checked in and found myself a corner, giving a few nods to people along the way. I still didn't know what Brondum looked like.

Finally, we made our way out into the Georgia Tech building. Its giant Dutch-barn construction towered high above the pool, making the high diving platform look like an upended matchbox. The enormous mercury-vapour lamps casting a hard brilliant light made the pool look like glacial meltwater. The stand of 13,000 was packed and noisy and lit by the golden sun pouring in through the side-less building.

I stood behind Lane 2 and made myself ready. All competitors were announced and we were under the control of the starter. As I hit the water, I felt instantly far better than in the morning session and made good progress over the field on the first butterfly length. This was eroded on the backstroke with the faster qualifiers moving past me. I was pushing harder than I should have and was outside of a good pacing pattern, but I had to stay with the field on the breaststroke. Out of the final turn my lungs began to scream with pain. Trying to switch them off, I stuck with Holger Kimmig of Germany as we battled down the final length. He got the touch but I had won bronze.

Hadn't I?

I finished fourth. Over the far side of the pool Jason Wenning of the USA had finished in second, leaving Kimmig with the bronze. I really thought I had done enough and dragged myself from the water. As I made my way back to the changing room boos started rumbling around the spectator stand. In his rolling southern accent the announcer said, 'Well folks, we have a scoreboard correction for you after that race.' I looked at the massive screen at the far end, next to 'Jason Wenning USA' the time had been replaced with 'DQ' – disqualified. Kimmig moved into second behind Terblanche, moving me into bronze position. I didn't feel I'd won it, somehow, but I could just about make out my family jumping up and down under the scoreboard, the only people happy with the news. I grinned as I was marshalled to the medallist pen.

That night you could cut the atmosphere in the flat with a knife. Chris had failed to defend one of his 1992 titles and was already thinking about the next. Of the eight guys in the flat, I was the only one who hadn't been to a Paralympics before.

Paralympic gold

My mind was racing with the force of a thousand wild horses. I couldn't stop it, catch it or divert it. The more I told myself I needed to sleep, the more awake I became. I tried setting myself problems to take my mind off the race, but as soon as I had thought of them I solved them. It was exactly the right state of mind but completely the wrong time. If it continued, I would be shattered for heats in the morning.

At 3 a.m. I decided to stop trying to fight my nerves and to work with them. If my mind wanted to swim, then that was what I would give it. So I rolled onto my back and began practising my butterfly technique. It calmed me instantly. I still was a mile off sleeping but all the time I could hear Mike saying 'process, not outcome . . .' and I repeated it to myself as a whispered mantra. I continued practising technique until 6 a.m., when it was time to get up.

In warm-up for the heats I felt superb. The 200-metre individual medley had blown out the cobwebs. I was in Heat 1 and Brondum in Heat 2. If I could win my heat in a new Paralympic record, that would really frighten him. As always, I warmed up: first on land, then easy swimming, then technique, then sprints, before some final high-quality slow swimming. I made my way to the call-up room; that was the first time I saw him. The same height as I was, though not as good-looking. He had two fingers missing from one hand, three from the other and a problem with both legs. I made my way to the same corner and sat waiting to be called. By now I was in autopilot. Out to my lane, tracksuit off and calm before the start.

With the bounce of the start signal I was away, not hitting the water but dividing it. I was controlled to the 50-metre halfway point, quick around the turn and working the kick as I drove off the wall. I pushed it hard, anxious to make a statement to Brondum. I touched the wall and turned to look to the far end of the pool. The huge scoreboard read, 'Giles Long, Great Britain, 1:10.38, New Paralympic Record'. I hoped it was enough. Ignoring the marshals, I stood on the poolside to watch his race.

Brondum looked really good in his heat and turned nearly three-quarters of a second more quickly than I did. When he finished, the same scoreboard said, 'Emil Brondum, Denmark, 1:10.24, New Paralympic Record'. I had been the Paralympic record holder for approximately four minutes and fifteen seconds. As the phrase goes, know your enemy. There had been a chink in Brondum's otherwise faultless 100-metre butterfly. In the final 5 metres I noticed he slowed ever so slightly. I walked away from the pool and muttered, 'If I'm gonna win this thing, that's where it'll be done.'

When I got back to my room at the athletes' village I couldn't help but feel annoyed with myself. I had pinned so much on frightening him with the Paralympic record. Instead, he was frightening me with a weapon I should have never given him in the first place. When I restarted swimming, I had told myself to be the best I could be, so what was I concentrating on when it really mattered?

I had spent years training for this. It was time to pay attention to that training. I would have to let him swim away from me down the first length, preserving my energy for the finish. It was a risky strategy to use over a race of 100 metres, but I had nothing else. This was it. I spent the middle of the day rehearsing it in my mind: how I wouldn't panic when I saw him in front of me at the turn and how I would throw every last ounce of life I had into it. Chris's bedside clock ticked away on a countdown.

I don't remember walking to the pool, warming up or getting to the marshalling area. Suddenly I was in the call-up room and sitting in the Lane 5 seat awaiting the start of the race, repeating my race plan slowly, accurately and calmly in my mind.

Suddenly there he was. Emil Brondum was standing in front of me with his toes almost on top of mine as he glowered into my eyes. We stared at each other. It was the first time since I was a kid that someone had tried to psych me out. He then started twisting his torso, flailing his arms out. 'Are you really that worried, mate?' I thought.

Five minutes later we were walking out. I looked over to the cheering crowd, the noise a distant buzz. But I heard the build-up clearly. 'Well, folks, we have an absolute showdown for you next in the men's S8 100-metres butterfly. The Paralympic record went not once but twice across the heats of this morning.' We stood behind our lanes, Brondum in 4, me in 5. The announcer made his way down the lane order stating the name, country and past achievements of each competitor. I had to shut out everyone else, repeating, 'Out fast, but not maximum – and don't panic.'

We were under starter's orders, and my heart rate was so hard that it could have broken my ribs from the inside. With the start signal, I moved like lightning and in the water I felt long and rangy, efficient and smooth. I stuck to my plan with the temptation to go absolutely flat out whispering in my ear all the way. At 45 metres I saw the wall. Five metres and I'd be able to gauge fully how much ground I had to make up. But a full metre from the wall I saw Brondum going the other way. I spun round the turn. The chase was on; my only hope was that I hadn't overcooked the books.

I pulsed a hard kick off the wall and started swimming at absolute maximum. Urging myself on all the way. With 25 metres to go, I had barely closed the gap at all. I started to feel a fury that I had never experienced before. My mind was screaming, 'No way am I losing this.' We entered the final 10 metres and the gap started to close. The plan was beginning to work. Then into the final five. We were level. My lungs felt as if they were bleeding. Every last muscle was spent and I was in agony. I held my breath and in the final stroke flung my arm forward.

Where had I finished? Had I won? I looked round and squinted to make out the scoreboard against the evening sun. It was a double whammy. I was first and reclaimed the Paralympic record with a time of 1:09.80. The pain of the race ebbed away like a galloping spring tide. In its place flowed rivers of ecstasy.

The medal ceremony was surreal. My gold medal was presented to me by teary eyed Dr Adrian Whiteson, president of the British Paralympic Association. Thirteen thousand people stood as the Union Flag was raised to the strains of the national anthem. I was in a daze. Just as I started a lap of honour around the pool, Adrian rushed over and shook my hand again. He was also chairman of the Teenage Cancer Trust.

Chapter Seven

Freefall and Failure

Unlike in the Olympics, swimming runs the full length of the Paralympics. On the final day of competition in Atlanta, the medal table was poised on a knife edge. The USA had an unassailable lead, with Australia having secured second place. But Great Britain and Germany both had 39 gold medals. They were going head to head in the final of the medley relay to secure third place overall.

Our team had finished first at the World Championships in Malta but were disqualified for a bad changeover between the first two swimmers. The German team benefited from our disqualification two years earlier and the line-ups were the same. Germany was stronger in the first half of the race; we were stronger in the second. As predicted, we initially lost ground. By the time it came for me to swim the butterfly leg, they had seven metres' lead on us. But I knew I was better than my opposite number and began taking chunks out of his lead. As I neared the wall I moved into a fixed-stroke pattern to give Marc Woods the best chance possible of predicting when I would hit the wall.

I'd reduced the deficit to just under 4 metres, putting Marc within range. He drove down the first 50 of the 100 metres like a man possessed, commandeering distance from Oliver Anders with every stroke. He planted his single foot on the wall and clawed back some more. He got closer as the two men neared the finish. Inside the final 3 metres, they drew level and hit the wall together. But it hadn't been quite enough. The German team had beaten us by 0.12 of a second. It remains one of the closest races in Paralympic history.

In Malta we had been disqualified because breast-stroker Iain Matthew had gone fractionally before Shaun Uren had touched the wall – called a flyer. We took the loss as a team and there was no animosity towards Iain, but in our disappointment we had not tackled the nuts and bolts of the relay mechanics until the day of the relay in Atlanta. It had been our undoing. All the talk (and shouting) had been 'Yeah! We're gonna win!' without ever talking through with one another how to make the team really sing as a unit. We were outcome before process. At the changeover between swimmers 1 and 2, we burned almost a whole second. Iain had been petrified of getting the team disqualified at world level again and had played it ultra-safe.

But it was us who had let him down by not picking

up on his fear and talking through it at any one of the many training camps or competitions that had occurred since Malta. A five-minute chat among four men could have easily raised the functioning of the team to make our first changeover just two-tenths quicker. A chance we didn't take. Again, it was an example of trying to make too great a change in too short a time. In the short term, the team were highly motivated by the excitement of the race, but as a team we hadn't been motivated to make sure that we were fast as a unit. Our Chimo Cycles had to coincide at the Paralympics, but we had never taken the time to capitalise on all the other times when they had come together to motivate us to take the hard steps to becoming better without becoming more risky.

Chris Holmes's games had got off to a shaky start, and in the first three days he haemorrhaged titles. Stories were being written in the press back home with headlines such as BRIDGE TOO FAR FOR HOLMES. But he had hit his strongest events halfway through the competition. He finished up with three golds, making him the most successful Paralympic athlete ever. We still laugh today about his ill-timed trip to the toilet, which coincided with my 100-metre butterfly. He listened in complete silence to the commentary and cheered so loudly when I won that the man in the next cubicle almost fell off the seat.

Homecoming hero

Returning home was an amazing experience. Mum and Dad returned a few days before me and the telephone had been ringing off the wall. Local press, radio and television all wanted to hear the story. When Mike first saw the three medals he was almost speechless and at first seemed unable to pick them up. As he delicately lifted the gold from its box he simply said, 'This is what it is all about.'

A deluge of invitations for receptions and parties began to arrive but there was still one final medical event on my agenda. In late August I booked into the RNOH for the final time. This time I was on an adult ward in a bed opposite an eccentric elderly gent called Dennis, who generously offered an impressive selection of rather *avant-garde* fruit cordials.

Watching the taped coverage of the games, I was shocked at how pronounced the dislocation had become in my right shoulder. The operation was to change the top half of the prosthesis and was a success. It was another major procedure but seemed so relaxed compared with the overbearing gloom of previous times.

This time would also incorporate a visit to see the Prime Minister: on the operating table on Monday, to the PM's house on Thursday.

I have been to 10 Downing Street on several occasions, but the only time I have been able to take a guest was the first time, when I went to the reception thrown by John Major. In the autumn of 1996 his government was beginning to go into meltdown, but despite this he was relaxed and charming. Joey came with me and thought it was hilarious when the National Heritage Secretary, Virginia Bottomley, congratulated him on his performance at the Paralympics. Although it was an easy mistake to make, he couldn't resist asking if she'd managed to watch much of the coverage.

John Major made an eloquent speech congratulating everyone and giving an insight into the history of Number 10. He then made his way around the room chatting to people as they got slowly sloshed on his booze. As left-leaning students, Joey and I decided to sort out a few things with the Conservative PM. The only problem was that neither of us had read a news-paper for approximately a year and, although every news story in the land implied that he was a bit thick, he proceeded to run intellectual rings round us. The evening rounded off fairly early with drunken athletes draped over every piece of furniture in the place demanding that it become a sleepover party. The Prime Minister thought it was all rather amusing. I think.

I decided I wanted to go to the Sydney 2000 Paralympics. I wanted to win the 100-metre butterfly and I wanted to set the world record in the final. But it was all too easy to forget how hard Paralympic training was. The invitations to parties and receptions kept coming and university was as good as it had ever been, and they were both brightly glittering areas of my life. Life was charging forward with exhilarating change, and there were breeding grounds of new ideas everywhere. Sadly, my swimming started to stagnate.

The Royal Family hosted an event at Buckingham Palace named 'A Celebration of British Sporting Life'. Every sporting celebrity was there: the Olympic and Paralympic teams, the England football, rugby and cricket teams, about a thousand guests in total. Chris had a VIP invitation, having won three golds in Atlanta, and pretended to be completely blind so that I could be his guide. We were ushered through ballrooms full of incredibly fit-looking individuals until we got to a smaller room full of famous faces. I gave Chris a running commentary of proceedings. At one point the Queen, Duke of Edinburgh, Prince Charles, Prince Edward and Princess Anne were all in the room. Chris and I were chatting to the boxer, Chris Eubank, who was dressed in riding gear with crop and monocle when Princess Anne wandered over. I pretended we knew each other and she went a mind-searching crimson. I explained that she had landed on my school playing field in a helicopter years earlier.

On the way back to Leeds I was buzzing with excitement. There'd been a sea change at the swimming club, too, as I was nominated to become City of Leeds Swimming Club Swimmer of the Year. Perhaps there would be a new beginning after all. I arrived at Leeds International Pool, where the award was to be presented.

Yorkshire people are diamond, and everyone bore a beaming smile as I made my way through the building and onto the poolside. However, soon after I received the prize, someone asked what I'd done to warrant the award. I realised that although there were lots of lovely people there, it was clear that unless the Paralympics gained the sort of coverage they deserved, some people were never going to understand the achievements of the athletes who competed in them.

Flatlining

In 1997 I pressed on with my studies, determined to leave with a 2:1 degree in geology. The successful operation had left my shoulders and my stroke looking much more even.

Each year for ten years after finally finishing chemotherapy in 1992, I would have one day when I would just break down in floods of tears. It would always be when things weren't quite going my way generally, and then I would catch a glimpse of myself in the mirror. The huge scar down my right arm reflected the well-worn path of the surgeon's knife; my shoulder was angular and ugly; and the remaining muscles looked as if they had been incorrectly rewired. I would always make sure that I was on my own when the clouds began to gather.

In 1997 that bleak day came just before the Easter

break. I had a letter from UCH, calling me back after a check-up. A chest X-ray had revealed a lump in my lung. I was gloomy rather than scared and shed tear after tear in my bedroom. I told my housemates, hoping to lighten the load, but their concerned faces crushed me further. So I hid behind a casual façade. My good friend Libby had not long lost her grandmother to a particularly cruel form of terminal cancer and came into my room in floods of tears. Somehow it made it easier to be strong.

The trip to London was a jittery one. I remembered the pact I had made with myself after being told I would have to fight the disease again. I smiled, shook my head and muttered 'idiot' to myself. As the radiographer took the chest X-ray I crossed my fingers. I kept them crossed until the consultancy with Dr Whelan, who had taken over from Professor Souhami. He jammed the X-ray onto the light box and peered at it. He took longer than normal and stood closer to the film than usual. After an agonising few moments, he announced that it was clear. It had all been a false alarm caused by a blood vessel in my lung that had been unexpectedly caught in cross section. I phoned my parents and then my housemates. Mum and Dad had a celebratory cup of tea. My housemates threw a party.

I trained the best I could but I was struggling with motivation. I knew what I wanted to do, but I seemed to be further away from winning *anything*, let alone the Paralympic gold. The sport wasn't inspiring me, and I was out of ideas about how to improve my performance at City of Leeds Swimming Club.

The final operation hit me harder than I thought it would and, with the additional pressure of final exams, I decided to miss the European Championships to be held that summer in Spain. Getting beaten by Brondum was a racing certainty and it was the last thing I wanted. I trained the best I could but wrote the season off competitively. Once again I needed small Chimo Cycles and not the unsustainably big Sydney dream.

In the summer of 1997 I graduated from the university with a 2:1. Needing a complete break, I went on holiday to Scotland with my girlfriend.

In concentrating on everything current I had completely neglected to plan for the future, especially in terms of earning money. Deciding to stay in Leeds, in an attempt to get my swimming back on track, I began looking for temporary work and trawled the temp agencies.

Chimo at work

Many of my friends were in a similar situation, having finished university thinking they were going to be instantly employable, but finding that no one would even consider them without experience. Joey and

Libby worked at a mail-order garden-equipment company along with friends Stu and Mido. Between them they spun a hugely successful campaign and got me a job, too. It was great fun at first, selling composting bins over the phone while messing about with your friends. People would phone up complaining about all sorts of things. I let my imagination run riot and in turn I would offer weird and wonderful solutions to their problems.

From there I went to the General, Municipal, Boilermakers and Allied Trade Union, better known as just the GMB. It was a funny place where people reacted to me in one of three ways: most people were friendly and content; some were actively hostile to the bourgeois graduate invading their space; and a few used me as a secret sounding board. It was the final group who were the most interesting. All were taking courses or thinking about applying and looking to better themselves. I guess they spoke to me because I had been to university and therefore apparently valued attainment. The secrecy was born from their fear that those who were hostile towards me would direct that same venom at them.

The risk for them was a lot greater. I was a temp who would be gone in a couple of months; the secret improvers might be there for much longer. It was when one of the hostiles let slip that they'd like to be a secret improver that I realised for the first time that the fuel of demoralisation is guilt. There was a whole group of people who, deep down inside, did really want to be excited and motivated by their daily lives. Unfortunately, they were forever waiting for someone else to provide the spark for their Chimo Cycles. If they weren't trying to stop people in the real world from getting on with theirs, they were cheering on highly motivated celebrities in magazines.

It was tiring, working nine to five and fitting in early-morning and evening training sessions. I now hated going to the pool and carried on as if on autopilot. I think that if I had stopped to consider why I was doing it I would have quit. After the disastrous results of the Atlanta 1996 Olympic team the government had set up the National Lottery, and sport was one of the named good causes. It would be the first time that British athletes could compete on an even footing with their competitors around the world. Unfortunately, the original legislation had been drafted to prevent any one individual from receiving money.

Then one morning in January 1998 the phone rang and the voice on the other end said, 'Hello, is that Giles? This is Jackie Quantock from Legal and General.' The previous summer a client of Dad's had been installing a new café for Legal and General at their headquarters. He had regular contact with the CEO, so I gave him a sponsorship proposal. In the following months I assumed the lead was dead. Conversely, Jackie came up to Leeds and took me out for lunch. Two hours later, we had hammered out a deal. It wasn't for a lot of money but it eased the financial pressure on a bank account laden with student debt.

Various sporting bodies were starting to establish themselves. Central to all of them was UK Sport, the government's Lottery-funding link to the sporting world. Until now, all full-time swimmers had competed on the dole. However, the cascade of cash just wasn't happening quickly enough.

The Legal and General money allowed me to work part-time. I asked the Leeds coach if I could train with his group for some of the more sparsely attended after-noon sessions. The answer was the same as ever but he did arrange for me to have a lane to train in before A1 got in. It was a positive step, as many of the A2 sessions were late in the evening, which left a short recovery time before training the next morning. I bought myself a fax machine and swam sessions that were written by Mike in Braintree. It felt crushing every time the A1 group came in and I was finishing off my session alone.

The money from Legal and General also paid for me to train in Philadelphia with an Olympic instructor for ten days. On Day 3 he had everyone in the pool towing five-gallon paint buckets. The stop/start motion created by the colossal drag tore my left shoulder to shreds.

When I got back to Leeds I saw the head coach on the poolside and explained what had happened. Maybe I'd worked alone for so long that I'd got into the habit of making my own plans – I can't remember whether I'd told him all the details about the programme – but he seemed surprised that I'd gone into it at all. I realised once and for all that I wouldn't be able to become a member of the team I so desperately wanted to join. I was the only disabled swimmer in the club and even though I had had many successes I had done so pretty much on my own because I couldn't fit into the training programme of the A1 swimmers. I felt excluded, but the truth was it could never work without the club significantly overhauling their training schedule, and this was something that simply wasn't going to happen.

Plummeting performance

I knew I had to leave but I was in such a motivational rut that I didn't know where to start. There were just four short months to go to the World Championships in Christchurch, New Zealand. I was still a top-level swimmer but heading in the wrong direction. At the time I had no idea just how quickly I was heading in that direction. There are lots of ways to motivate yourself, of which Chimo is one. Panic and fear are others, and you can live in that state, but getting the outcome you desire becomes chance rather than design.

In qualification my times were lacklustre across the board. Each race was a battle and nothing flowed. Dad was with me in Sheffield and we exchanged disappointed expressions all weekend, trying last-minute changes to eke out a few extra tenths – a strategy that rarely works. But I was on the team, and that was at least a basis for constructing a way forward. That summer the first ever Lottery-funded trip sent the British Disability Swimming Team to Florida for a training camp.

The entire operation crossed from amateur to professional. We had our own medical staff, there was no problem getting enough coaches out or enough pool time. There were a lot of new faces on the team and most were a bit shy, but one stood out from the crowd. Ritchie Barber was from Salford in Manchester and talked as if he worked for the Tourist Board. In his Mancunian drawl, he had the entire team in stitches for most of the time. The unusual combination of the Florida sunshine and his ready humour were enough to keep any team pressing on through the training-camp blues. His humour out of the pool was matched by his work ethic within it. Watching him absorbed in his training flicked in me a glimmer of a memory of how I used to enjoy swimming. I wanted to reach out and grab it, but it was as if I'd forgotten how to or had just lost the ability.

When we got back to the UK, I sought a new beginning. I left City of Leeds Swimming Club and moved back in with my parents in Braintree. The three months of training I had there were poorly structured and erratic. Mike had moved jobs within the local council and could no longer get pool time. I flew out to Club La Santa in Lanzarote at the last minute to get some quality long-course metres in, but, without a coach there, my main strength – that of good technique – remained as stagnant as it had in all the time post-Atlanta. The change of moving out of the Leeds Swimming Club system had given me a ton of new ideas and motivation, but I was harvesting the problems of poor preparation.

Coming second

When we departed Heathrow in mid-October for the holding camp in Brisbane, everyone looked excited and happy. I felt excited, too, but also hollow – a traveller going with the team to make a stab at success rather than a heavyweight linchpin and a gold-medal contender. In Australia, I still couldn't get it right. The body has a series of fitness types that can be thought of as gears. I felt as if I had gears one and five; each time I tried to accelerate I couldn't do it smoothly. The inefficiencies brought about by my technical flaws and lack of specific fitness were costing valuable time.

The team were functioning well but unsure of the new management. Few relationships had time to form before the second-biggest meet across the four-year cycle. When we landed in New Zealand and made it to the hotel, it was very late. That was where I met up with my roommate Marc Woods. He had elected to miss the holding camp in Australia and fly straight to Christchurch. He had the same form of cancer as I did, though in his ankle, and I regard him as an incredibly inspirational man.

People seemed at their peak, as they should do, but I felt far from my best. It was the same story as it had been for months: I had speed but was inefficient.

The competition started and began following a carbon copy of the programme two years before at the Paralympics. My performance in the 200-metre medley on the first day is a painful memory. Having scraped through the heats, I qualified sixth and felt there was nothing more to give in the final. There wasn't and I finished seventh overall.

The next day was the butterfly. I spent that night guzzling carbohydrate drink and re-shaving down, clutching at straws to save the day. That evening I had no nerves and slept all the night.

Due to my poor entry time, I was third fastest on the start sheet and in the same heat as Brondum. Because I had missed the Europeans the previous year, he had thought I had retired, but there was not enough surprise in the world to give me the edge in this race. He qualified – easily fastest enough for the final. I went through second, though only just ahead of Ben Austin of Australia.

There was no extra spark for the final. In truth there was no spark at all. I sat in the call-up room feeling thoroughly ashamed. I was going to let everyone there down and, even worse, everyone at home who supported me.

We made our way out to behind our lanes. Brondum

looked mentally right and excited by the prospect of the final. I genuinely didn't care. Before I knew what was happening, the gun had gone and I was in the water. I was flat out at 30 metres and with 70 to go I knew it was going to be a painful one. As I approached the turn I saw Brondum going the other way with exactly the same lead he'd had over me in Atlanta. I tried to fight, but inside I couldn't. With a full 45 metres to go I knew I was beaten and it was agony. The second length seemed to take an age, as the tears streaming from my eyes slowly filled my goggles.

With my lungs burning I looked up at the scoreboard and was dismayed with the time. At just over a second outside my best it was a disgrace. It was compounded by the fact that Brondum had gone faster than my time in Atlanta. I was in the unusual situation of having a standing record that was set prior to a rule change. He hadn't broken the official world record but, since I wasn't allowed to swim that way any more, his time was as good as.

From that point on, Great Britain started losing medals left, right and centre. Golds became silvers, silvers became bronzes and bronzes became minor places. Relays that we had once dominated made way to a new order. I left it two days before phoning my parents with the news.

On the long flight home from New Zealand I had a long time to think about what had gone wrong. I asked myself over and over, 'Why has this happened? Why have you let this happen?' In truth I knew why it had happened: it was because I hadn't been swimming enough and training to the standard required for top-level competition. But, even after all that had happened, there was something inside me that just kept saying, 'Yes, but you love swimming.'

Marc had told me of a tool that he used to get himself to the pool when he didn't want to go. He had a whole list of reasons in his head why he liked swimming. At the top of the list were the primary reasons, the ones that had started him swimming initially. As he worked his way down towards the bottom they started to become arguably more trivial, but on certain days more tangible. Things such as being able to eat what you want and not put on weight.

It was a great tool for a motivated athlete in a good programme who needed a push over the edge on a tough day. But my motivation had hit complete rock bottom. I felt I was comatose. But deep down I knew I still loved it, and that was something. It was the faint pulse that told me I still wanted to do it. That was the most important thing of all. With that I proved to myself that I wanted to look for anything that might spark a change and a minute Chimo Cycle.

One member of the team who hadn't swum badly was Ritchie. He had won the S7 50-metre butterfly and broken the world record. The team had gone crazy with admiration. I asked him about joining City of Salford Swimming Club. We were back in Britain in late November and within three days I was up in Manchester.

Chapter Eight

Renaissance

At home I felt a twisting pain every time I explained to people around me that I had lost the number-one spot. The disappointment in their faces was harder than any disenchantment I felt. It hadn't been a heroic defeat; I hadn't gone down in a blaze of others' glory. It had been a miserable sequence of preventable catastrophes and the end result was a silver medal – not so much a silver medal won as a gold medal lost.

Perhaps it seems flippant to regard a silver medal from the World Championships like that. A medal proves that in a certain race, in a certain sport, on a certain day, the winner was the best. The bigger, shinier and heavier the medal, the better they are. These are the medals I love to show people.

For me, they are also a representation of personal endeavour, perseverance and determination. I couldn't honestly say there was much of any of those qualities in the medals I brought back, so I never show them to anyone.

It was a case of *déjà vu* when I first arrived at the City of Salford Swimming Club in Broughton, just north of Manchester city centre. Colin Hood was the coach of an elite group of senior swimmers who sat alongside the main top squad. His was the group I needed to be in. He was clearly apprehensive at first at having a swimmer with a disability in his group. There was more than enough space in the pool but it was unknown territory.

Colin didn't dismiss the idea out of hand. Instead, he agreed to look at me for a few initial sessions. Ritchie's Mum, Nikki, let me stay while I found my feet at the new club. Colin and I came to an arrangement. He would let me stay in for the first half of each session before I had to move out to train with a lower group. We got on well and after just four sessions he let me stay in.

The group of just ten people seemed to function in a way that I had forgotten even existed. People were more than friendly. They were friends, which generated a superb atmosphere. There was also a fantastic work ethic among the swimmers. They were part of the overall club but also a separate unit. They were a collection of people who looked out for one other, in the pool, in the gym and on the street. Most important of all, I was an asset to the group. I was someone who could and would be allowed to make a contribution.

Hard questions

While getting my flat in Manchester sorted, I had spent a lot of miles on the road and plenty of time to ponder my disappointment at the World Championships about why I had gone from an improving swimmer on the way up to one in decline. I kept asking myself where all the motivation had gone. Why did my passion for the sport I had loved so much wither to the point of desolation? While looking towards the new mountaintop of the Sydney games, I had forgotten how hard the climb was to reach the Atlanta summit. I had let stagnation take hold, had no Chimo to hand to stir the waters. I had also been distracted by other people's mountaintops – watching other people utilising their Chimo Cycles doesn't necessarily engage you in yours.

With a rented flat in Worsley, a National Lottery grant from UK Sport (which had been set up to administer Lottery funding) and sponsorship from Legal and General, the future was bright. I was never going to be rich but I could pay the rent and the bills, run my car and pursue my swimming ambitions, all within a place that wanted to have me, where I was adding value.

Every member of the squad had achieved in the pool. There were national champions, GB team members and competitors from the Commonwealth Games. There wasn't a single person there you couldn't like. As I rebuilt all the gaps in my strength and fitness levels, I began to form a strong friendship with Adrian Turner, or Adi, who remains one of my closest friends today.

He loved comedy and was the perfect foil for my undergraduate humour. He was also a source of inspiration to me. I had never seen a swimmer able to push themselves so phenomenally hard. As it turned out, a year later it was a quality that would nearly kill him. Every training session he reminded me how much dedication I'd had before I had started to lose motivation.

Colin's style of coaching was one that I had never experienced before and for me still sets a benchmark. He was the team leader, though he was never detached. There are many styles of good leadership, but I feel the most effective is possessed by the person who lives every second with other members. In sport, the line between coach and athlete is pronounced: the coach orders, the athlete does. In swimming the coach stands on the side, above the swimmer; they are dry and never out of breath. So it's incredibly difficult for the swimmer to take advice.

But on tough sets Colin seemed to share our pain. If we'd done badly he didn't shout. Instead he would be visibly disappointed, as we were. If we had done the job well he would appear genuinely excited as he recorded our times in his book. His style of coaching inspired me to push myself in every training session.

When I was training at the limit, thoughts would dance through my mind. As my pulse rate went up and up and lungs began to suck air in like a vacuum cleaner, I would think, 'I can't go on.' Each time I came close to easing off I would have the counterthought, 'Don't let him down, you can't let Colin down.'

The flat I was renting was lovely despite the night-time antics of neighbours. But it was close to the M62 and the increased level of pollution, combined with the additional moisture of the Manchester air, began to cause breathing problems. I went to my local doctor and after a quick peak-flow test was prescribed two forms of inhaler. Problem solved.

Training camps in Australia were becoming more common as the money pumped in by the government was used to harden potential Olympians and Paralympians to climate change and jetlag. Getting sunburned or dehydrated even by 1 per cent could lead to a 10 per cent drop in performance – more than enough to put you out of a final.

Every four or five weeks Dad would come up to Manchester to check on my technique. There simply was no one else at the time who understood the intricacies of the timing. Most of it translated directly from able-bodied butterfly, but the final tweaks that really made the stroke fire were unique to swimming it with one arm. He and Colin got on extremely well and started to learn from each other, forming a powerful alliance that I could draw on.

The USA opens its competitions to foreign teams only in odd-numbered years – the years in which the Paralympics and World Championships are *not* held. This is an effort to try to conceal the kind of form their athletes are in and introduce an element of surprise. It doesn't really work, because they publish the results on the Internet! Go figure, as the Americans would say. In the late spring of 1999 a large team from Great Britain flew out to Arizona for a training camp and competition in Phoenix. It was one of the best competitions I have ever been to. On the hottest day the temperature hit 49°C, every sunset was sublime and no one on Earth opens a swim meet like the Americans.

Back to work

I've seen ostentatious openings before but this exceeded them all. There was space for the spectators down one side of the pool with competitors down the other under sunshades. As with most meets, there is never quite enough space, so inevitably there were pieces of equipment, false limbs, wheelchairs and various assorted bits of paraphernalia strewn around the poolside. As the scarlet light of the Arizona sunset began to hit the giant Saguaro cacti around the pool, a man wearing a Stars and Stripes shirt appeared at the far end of the pool mounted on a white horse. The crowd fell silent as the horse slowly rounded the pool. At the scoreboard end it became apparent that this beast was utterly enormous and, to judge by the complete disarray of the competitors, you could be forgiven for assuming that most people thought he was going to stop. Instead, as it rounded the top corner, the horse broke into a canter and came charging down the poolside to a load of competitors all suddenly searching for false limbs and wheelchairs. People were running away on legs that were either too small or too large; some were making an escape using a wheelchair without a seat; and everyone else was just falling over whatever was left. Having caused complete pandemonium, the rider stood up in the stirrups, played the American national anthem on a miniature trumpet and left.

I won the 100-metre butterfly with ease, coming close to Andrew Haley of Canada, who swam in the S9 class. The meet helped me stamp authority over one key rival. Ben Austin from Australia was a young swimmer on the way up and I needed to keep an eye on him. He'd got the better of me in the 200-metre IM twice before. Usually, he passed me doing breaststroke, but this time, when we hit the 150-metre mark, I had about a metre on him and kept it that way.

The training camp that followed was also a great success, though the Arizona climate could be a cruel mistress. Once, the pool was double-booked and we were bumped to a training slot in the middle of the day.

We were scheduled to swim an overload set and begged the coaches to let us postpone it until the evening. They said no way. Everyone in the team got angry as the sun tore out of the sky and the work rate went up. Our point was proved when one of the team passed out through exhaustion – and that was a coach.

That summer the European Championships were held in Braunschweig (Brunswick), Germany, and co-incided with the first full solar eclipse to pass over Europe in decades. Whether it was a good or bad omen didn't matter. The training at Salford was paying off in spades, as I won the 200-metre IM on the first day of competition and then the 100-metre butterfly on the second. Brondum wasn't there but the time I posted was quick. I knew he'd be watching and I knew it would rattle him.

Donna Liley, a freelance journalist, managed to get me some work experience with BBC Radio 5 Live. She'd got me six weeks' work as a researcher within a small team under the direction of an avid Leicester City supporter called Ian Bent. I researched a piece on free diving, a little-known sport at the time, and a piece on chess. At the outset, it seemed fairly innocuous until you consider that people were being murdered in its name. Ian's team also shared an office with *The Mark and Lard Show* on Radio 1 and I worked for them for a spell too and got to meet the great Peter Kay before his career took off.

As time marched on, the squad became even more

of a unit, so much so that, when I was selected to go to Australia to swim at the Southern Cross Games and everyone else went to Bethune in France, I felt as if I was missing out. After three weeks of muscle-deadening training on the Gold Coast, we flew down to Sydney. Everyone was tired and nothing was expected in terms of results. The key aim of entering the competition was to swim in the Sydney 2000 pool.

I raced as hard as I could for every single event. Although I was incredibly tired, my times were vastly better than I expected. From the very first moment I dived in I felt excited to be there.

Christmas catastrophe

The Salford team were getting on so well that we all decided to go away for a couple of days to party just before Christmas. Colin had a programme that started on the day after Boxing Day and wanted us to have a few days off. Adi and I found an incredible pair of houses on the coast in Oban, on Scotland's west coast. When we arrived the sea was like glass, unbothered by air that was still and crisp.

The first night Adi had gone to bed early and appeared to be coming down with flu. He had not long competed and was prone to getting ill after competitions, having pushed his body to its limit. All the same, we decided to call the doctor. She came, said it was flu and left.

His condition steadily worsened and within two hours we called the doctor back. This time she appeared more concerned but was still convinced it was flu.

As the night drew in we gradually retired to bed. I was so used to hearing the background hum of the city that the silence was eerie. In the early hours of the crow-black morning I heard a haunting call of 'Giles, Giles.' I thought I was going mad and tried to get back to sleep until I heard it again.

I opened the bathroom door to find Adi on the floor looking jaundice yellow and delirious, having hit his head on the sink. The doctor duly arrived about twenty minutes later at the isolated houses, this time with an ambulance, and Adi was admitted to hospital.

The holiday was followed in short order by my Nana's funeral. News about Adi just kept getting worse as he was transferred from Oban to Glasgow Central Hospital.

When we got back into training it was without Adi and the calendar seemed to shrink as Olympic and Paralympic Trials were in just four months' time. Before being ill, Adi had a good chance of making the Olympic team in the 200-metre and 400-metre IM. His having finally been diagnosed with a rare autoimmune disorder left his chances looking slender.

Swimming for the rest of the group continued as normal. I wanted to do more to ensure victory in Sydney. One method of improving performance was hypnosis. Previously, I had come into brief contact with a sport psychologist who knew how to do it, but I never really thought it was for me. It was only when I met Sheelagh Rodgers that it started to feel like something I could use to my benefit. Sheelagh had worked with the team around the time of the European Championships in Germany. I explained that I'd like to try hypnosis as a way of squeezing every last hundredth off my race time.

Over the course of just three sessions she taught me a transforming skill. The first session was all about finding the depth to which I could be hypnotised. It was a hell of an experience finding out. She put me into a trance by getting me to sit back on the sofa with my eyes closed as she counted backwards from ten. In between numbers she would add in a suggestion as to the level of relaxation I should be feeling. When she reached one she seemed to finish talking and not restart. From then on a series of dreamlike images flooded my mind. The image that I can clearly recall even today is that of two children sitting on a wall talking to each other. Never once did their mouths stop moving or pause for breath and with each new word their facial features would also change. Not their expressions, their features. Eventually, I heard a voice in the distance calling me back.

By the time we had the second session I had thought of a 'trigger phrase', which had to be easy to remember but rarely heard in everyday conversation. The less it was heard the more potent it would be. I chose 'increase the power'. She gave me a tape of the session, warning me not to listen to it in the car. The third time we listened to the tape together and I evaluated its uses.

As Olympic and Paralympic Trials drew ever closer, Adi still looked tired. He had lost a staggering amount of weight. He had been banned from the pool but had tried to sneak in a training session while Colin was out of town for a few days. But the head coach was one step in front of him, having briefed all the lifeguards to not let him in. He didn't even manage to put his bag down before they threw him out. It must have been frustrating beyond belief.

Increase the power

In March I flew with the GB Team to Denmark for one of the most important races of my career. The tiny meet in the beautiful castle town of Hillerod, just north of Copenhagen, was where Brondum and I would go head to head in the 100-metre butterfly in Paralympic year. Colin couldn't make it, so I was assigned to Ritchie's Mum, Nikki, herself an accomplished coach.

Colin knew how important it was for me to win this race and had tapered me for it, which he wouldn't have normally done. When I hit the chilly water I felt great and I knew within the first three strokes that I would be in with a chance of resetting the world record for the first time in almost six years.

Still, I had to remember not to use my magic phrase, 'increase the power'. That was for the games. It was extremely difficult *not* to think about it.

The race ran like clockwork. Unlike other knife-edge performances, I knew this one was in the bag with 75 metres still to go. As I headed home 'increase the power' just popped into my head. Who knows what effect it had? I touched the wall and spun round to see the time. The green numbers read '1:08.31 WR [world record]'. Brondum looked at the board and said, 'God, that's fast.' I thought, 'Gotcha!'

After clambering out, he slumped down in a chair and looked up to the ceiling with tears rolling down his face. I felt pretty mean and sat down next to him to commiserate. After the agony of the World Championships I couldn't take pleasure in watching anyone go through that. But as soon as he mentioned it was his birthday on the day of the 100-metre butterfly in Sydney I just had to walk away.

When I returned home there was no fanfare, no free car or media scrum. But that didn't matter. Seeing Colin's face beaming at a job well done was a great feeling and I felt like the legitimate holder of the record again. We set about planning for the trials, though with a world record in the bag it should just be a formality. Dad continued to come up to see me train and correct minor defects that emerged as tough sets pulled my stroke out.

With a few weeks to go to trials, I arrived for training

and wandered in to the changing rooms to get ready. Adi arrived not long after, put his stuff on the bench and broke down in floods of tears. I felt excruciating empathy as he sat and said, 'I'm just not going to make it, G.' He had made an incredible recovery and bounced back to set some very respectable times. Unfortunately, his main chance was in the 400-metre IM, and this is the most unforgiving of events. It left him with an insurmountable task. His dreams lay at the wrecker's yard.

I told Colin what had happened and they spent much of the session sitting on the side talking things through. There aren't many coaches who could have even come close to the warmth Colin showed that day and there aren't that many swimmers who would wish someone the very best of luck when their own dreams were shattered. Adi called me the very next day to make sure that I gave it everything.

The trials turned out to be a formality and I qualified easily. So did Ritchie and Sarah Bailey, also a Paralympian at the Salford club. Training through August was difficult with everyone else in the club on holiday. Ritchie, Sarah and I were unflinching as we strove on. As the Olympics got under way the TV coverage was immense. Records tumbled in the pool with Ian Thorpe wowing the crowds every time he put a toe in the water.

When the Paralympic team arrived at the holding camp we were on autopilot. We'd experienced the travel, jetlag and climatic changes many times before. Colin was with us for the final run-up to the games to help soothe the nerves.

After a backbreaking flight in economy class, we landed in Brisbane, Australia. The Paralympic Games started in three weeks and my main event was twenty-two days away. Nothing was new: airport, aeroplane, plastic in-flight food, immigration, transfer, hotel check-in, hotel, pool, gym, roommate.

There were a lot of smiles but no one was flustered. There was only one person on the swimming team who had never competed in an international event before and the calm vibe emitted by the rest of the team was obviously rubbing off. Matt Crabb was here for the 400-metre freestyle and looked good to go.

I checked in with Chris Holmes, my roommate, and we made our way around the complex to unpack our kit.

Gold Coast

The pool was at St Hilda's private school on the Gold Coast. Glistening in the sun was the pool where I had carefully carved out metres on numerous trips before. This was second nature, too, as was the dread of getting an ear-infection. And if you don't wear sun cream you're going to fry. The evidence was all around at every training session as parents who looked like grandparents picked their kids up. I overheard one bronzed little boy ask his leathery mother, 'Why are all those people putting that cream on them?' She replied, 'That's 'cos they're from England and it always rains there.' I gave her a wry smile.

I stood behind my lane with the other swimmers while Colin outlined the warm-up routine for us. We all had goggles on and, as the pace clock hit twelve o'clock, the first swimmer led off. I didn't want to lead. It was no big deal; it was just a warm-up. But what if I'd somehow forgotten how to do it? It was ridiculous. I'd been a competition swimmer for thirteen years and gone to the Atlanta Paralympics, but there was still the slightest chance that on the plane I'd forgotten how to do it.

I dived in and felt absolutely abysmal. My hands were skating all over the place and, only two days before, they had been locking in the water like an oarsman's blades. My body felt heavy, as if every vessel were lined with lead, and my heart rate was soaring. This was an easy training session. If Colin had written it up at home I might have looked at it and thought it was so easy as to be a bit boring. But I was panicking and down-beat within twenty minutes of having started. I stood at the end of the pool as Chris finished the set he was on. He looked up and said, 'How're you feeling, G-ster?'

'Awful.' I responded in a dark tone, which clearly

annoyed him a bit because his response was firm. 'You've just flown halfway around, jumped in a pool in this blistering sun and this bloody pool's got about half an inch of sun cream floating on it. You're not supposed to feel good, you know that. Concentrate on feeling good in three weeks' time!'

With that he pushed off the wall and left me to think about it. I looked up at Colin on the poolside. He smiled, raised his eyebrows and nodded. So I got on with it.

I really struggled with the jetlag. During the daytime my bed was like a siren, calling me to have a little lie-down, coaxing me across the room to make sure it was still as good as the last time. At nighttime, it turned into a torture chamber. It was either too hot or too cold. I wanted to be a serenely sleeping Goldilocks but I was more like a bear with a sore head.

Those small hours seemed to draw out for ever, with a thousand thoughts flying around my head. I would revert to what I had thought before my race in Atlanta – go when the gun sounds, kick underwater and get the first three strokes right. It was simple and robust. If you have just three things to think about you can turn your head into a mental fortress. The problem is it can also get a bit a dull thinking that over and over and over. When that happened either Chris or I would quietly say, 'Are you awake?' We gave each other the response that always made us laugh. 'Of *course* I fucking am!' I knew it was coming but it still made me jump sky-high every single time.

Bet fair

If you put a load of bored people together in a hotel on the outskirts of town and they've all got energy levels going through the roof, sooner or later they're going to get up to something. This is a highly focused group of people, also highly competitive. After training, over breakfast I got into a heated discussion about the number of lengths that someone could do underwater in the small pool behind our apartment block at the hotel. It wasn't very big, about 11–12 metres long, and I said it would be easy to do six lengths. Most people weren't having any of it, but the bravado was building on all sides. Then Matt Crabb put $60 on the table and said, 'Sixty says you can't.' Now, getting sucked into macho betting is something that should be left to complete idiots who can't handle peer pressure. But by this time lots of other people were standing around, so I shook his hand and took the bet.

We made our way down to the kidney-shaped pool with what was now half the swimming team in tow. I got ready and got in. Colin turned up, too. I thought he wasn't going to be all that impressed with my antics so close to a major championships, but instead he seemed just as entertained as everyone else. Matt put his sixty on the side of the pool next to mine. We agreed a two-length warm-up. I put my goggles on and dipped my head under the water to push off.

To my complete horror the water was like milk. I pushed off the wall and crashed straight into another wall. The sides of the wretched kidney pool were curved at every point, so navigation was near impossible. This was going to be the quickest $60 I'd ever spent. I put my head above the surface and everyone was in hysterics. Anyway my warm-up was over, this was it. I decided on a slightly different tactic: rather than try to swim in a straight line across the bow of the kidney I would swim around its curvature. I reckoned that this would add about a metre to each length and probably bring the total to about 68 metres without a breath.

I drew in a series of deep breaths and to the sound of cheers from the crowd I bobbed my head under and began. The first two lengths were a cinch and the third was OK, but, as I turned underwater onto the fourth, my lungs started that too familiar feeling. I had felt it hundreds of times before, gasping for air in the final few metres of the race. By the end of the fourth length I was in trouble. My lungs were screaming and my heart was about to pop out and start dancing on my chest.

I turned onto the fifth length thinking that I may well have to throw the race. But as I did so I repeated the phrase that I'd practised with Sheelagh in the hypnotism sessions. In my head, and 'hearing' it in my own voice, I said clearly and without tonal variation, 'Increase the power.' The screaming in my lungs just ebbed away and my heart seemed to become a burbling engine. My body was still being pushed but it seemed so manageable. I touched the wall after my sixth length and as I stuck my head above the water to draw breath it was like breaking a spell. My lungs sucked in air while my heart beat a war drum in my brain.

I was feeling confident, or more certain, perhaps – not because of winning the bet but because I'd proved to myself that I had a secret weapon. Hypnotism worked and I could turn it on at the point in a race that I needed to squash any pain that might slow me down. With that, I collected the money and took everyone to the bar for a drink. Not really, I just kept it.

That afternoon it was back to business. I was feeling better mentally. Chris, unfortunately, was going the other way. Sydney was to be his fourth Paralympics and in the previous three he'd won enough medals to make him, at the time, Britain's most successful Paralympian ever. But for him this time round there was more than just intense competition. Several onlookers, myself included, felt that someone he was racing had been wrongly classified and was enjoying an inappropriate advantage.

I felt it was eating away at Chris and that in turn was starting to eat away at me. By this stage we were just ten days away from the start of the games and just one week away from flying down to Sydney. I tried to keep on top of my positive state of mind by engaging in witty banter.

In the pool I was beginning to feel on song. All I needed was the final sparkle to my form. But a new problem had emerged. There was a delay in getting fast-skins from Speedo. These are high-performance racing suits that come in various cuts. They had been released onto the market just before the Sydney games and every competitive swimmer in the world wanted to race in one. But there just wasn't enough of the 'sharkskin' fabric to make them. It was a bit of commercial realism that had never hit the team so directly before. The Olympic team were fully kitted out but we couldn't get our hands on them. Some of the coaches managed to get Olympic team members to give theirs up. They had done their swimming and didn't need them any more. If I had been asked to give up the suit that I'd worked so hard to get I'm not entirely sure that I would have.

Eventually, a handful turned up just before we were due to fly to Sydney. I wanted a cut called a leg skin; it covers the whole of your legs from hip to ankle. I got just one. The perishable nature of the suit meant that it would give me one trial and the final only. One sharp nail tear and it would be back to ordinary trunks. I wrapped it up carefully and took it back to my room. That evening the team manager revealed that, due to a problem with the sponsorship contract, we had to strip the brand name from all of the bodysuits. It meant handing all the bodysuits back leaving the poor medical staff to sit up all night removing the logo transfers with nail-polish remover.

Sporting celebration

Australia's connection with sport is like no other nation's on the planet. When the 2000 Olympics had been packed away for another four years, there had been a national sense of mourning. But with the impending Paralympics the whole place sprang into overdrive again. Everywhere you looked there were flags and banners. It was how in childhood I'd imagined competing in the games would be.

Chris had always been a fantastic steadying force throughout my international career and I had grown used to that. But he was fighting demons on this occasion. I didn't have the skills to be able to turn him round mentally and so had to try to stay out of his way. I couldn't imagine a situation where I could be more ruthless. It was either that or risk all that I'd worked to claw back.

With the opening ceremony just a matter of hours away, I nearly threw it all away over the most trivial of mistakes. After a light training session in the Sydney Aquatic Centre, I stood waiting for the bus with Glen Lindsay, a brilliant physio who had been working with the team for some time. I was wearing sandals, which

I didn't normally do, and agreed to walk the half-mile back to the village with him. When I woke up the next morning, my calves were unbelievably sore and felt as if they were going to explode. Having practised everything down to the very last thoughts I would have before each stage, I had lost concentration at a seemingly innocuous time and it had blown up into a potential nightmare. How could I have been so careless? Glen got to work on them.

The Sydney opening ceremony was every bit as exciting as Atlanta. As we walked around the stadium with giant walls of cheering people to either side, we decided to throw some of the pin badges we'd been given into the crowd. We hadn't anticipated the strength of the wind and we stopped throwing them when they whipped back in our faces.

If athletes are competing close to the opening ceremony they will often miss it. It seems a crying shame if you've worked so hard to get there that you can't burn each and every detail of the experience into your memory. But you have to ask yourself why you are there. Is it to win a race or to enjoy the spectacle? After all, there will be many games equally as spectacular after yours in which you could be a crowd member rather than a competitor. But I found that the boost of adrenalin the opening show provided induced such a powerful and inspirational euphoria that I never missed it.

The very next day was my 200-metre IM. The first

day of competition was twitchy for everyone. Bus stops filled earlier than expected as everyone left extra time as a contingency. In the warm-up, I felt sharp, especially at the front end of my butterfly, which was something Colin and I had honed. He loved cricket and we spent hours using a palm-sized 1-kilo medicine ball. I would lie on my back and throw it to him and he accurately returned it though standing metres away.

The marshalling process was simple and the call-up room compact, with competitors sitting in rows all facing a series of windows with half-tilted Venetian blinds, through which they could see that the only thing separating the tiny room from the wall of twenty thousand people sitting opposite was a thin stretch of water.

As the race started I felt good. I worked the butterfly on the way out and spun round the turn into the backstroke. Both other strokes also felt strong and, as I finished, I looked to the scoreboard expecting to see a good time and easy qualification for the final. The time was so beyond awful it was embarrassing. To have made it to that level and be so far off the mark was unforgivable. I would be lucky to make the final at all.

With the passing of the next two heats I tried to keep a mental tally of where I was in the overall standings. My relief was palpable as the scoreboard flashed up my name. I'd made the final, though only just, scraping in by a few tenths of a second to qualify seventh fastest. It put me in Lane 1 and was a wake-up call. I went back to my room in the athletes' village and mentally stepped it up a notch.

Going full tilt

I decided that, if I was going to win a medal, I would have to be going at full tilt straight from the gun. I spent the day drilling my mind to accept that the evening's racing was going to be incredibly painful. Lance Armstrong, the seven-times Tour de France winner, once said, 'Pain is temporary, quitting lasts a lifetime.' I adopted the mantra, 'It's two minutes forty of pain or lifetime of agony.'

I had never been in an outside lane at a major championship before. As I led the other seven competitors across behind the blocks it felt like an advantage, a secret weapon. They would have written me off after my heat swim.

My muscles flicked like a switch when I heard the start signal. I pierced the surface and began swimming demonically. I hit the wall in the same time as my 100-metre butterfly world record split and powered down the backstroke 50 metres. I could hear my lungs wheezing underwater and thought they were going to explode as I turned onto the breaststroke – they don't call it the lung-buster for nothing. At the 150-metre mark I was in total overdrive before downing the final freestyle 50 metres to the finish.

It had been a massive personal best for me but I had come fourth. The time of 2:40.01 would have won the gold medal in Atlanta. I had been in the lead three-quarters of the way through the race.

I trudged back up to the rest of the team not even knowing who had won, I was so disappointed. Marc congratulated me with a big grin. 'The gutsiest swim I've ever seen, mate,' he said, making me feel a whole lot better. The one person I hadn't spoken to was Colin. He was leaning over the railing looking at the splits of the race. It was the only time I'd ever seen him look disappointed from a personal best. I said, 'Tomorrow's our day, Col.'

He nodded slowly and said, 'I hope so.'

Back at my room I listened to my hypnosis tape for the last time.

Race day

The following morning I was the only person up; everyone else had a rest day. Sleep had been inconsistent but not as anxious as four years previously. As I shaved, I looked at myself in the mirror. My face had a hard edge to it. I put my nose an inch from the mirror, looked myself right down the very centre of each pupil and said, 'You deserve this.' I picked up my bag and left.

There was none of the schoolboy tactics in the

call-up room before heats. I had felt razor sharp in the warm-up but something was wrong with my technique. The timing was slightly out and I couldn't isolate what was causing the problem. The heat swim was a formality and I went through in front of Brondum to lead the pack into the final. The morning session had passed with ruthless efficiency but, if my timing was out, it could cost me the gold.

I sat on my own in the food hall pondering what to do. To change anything in the warm-up before the Paralympic final would go completely against the grain; to change a technical detail would be lunacy.

That evening, the spectator stand in the swimming pool was packed to the rafters. I went through my race warm-up and tweaked the very front end of the pull, just changing the pitch of my hand ever so slightly. It had always been a major strength, to be able really to think about technical changes. Its downside was that sometimes I would overthink and try too hard. I tried to switch off. I also decided that I had spent the last two years chipping away incrementally at the world record and that I had done it through changing strokes fractionally over each length of every training session. With Dad and Colin, I had bullied my butterfly into shape with relentless practice. Part of the practice had been that of change. If I decided to change something, it would be nothing new. I'd got so used to using change as a motivational tool on a daily basis that I wasn't scared of it. Even just hours before the biggest race of my life.

As I sat in the call-up room, the familiar mix of excitement and terror began coursing through my veins and sparking down my nerves. Brondum sat to my right and Austin, who had beaten me the day before, to my left. I sat motionless, conscious that soon I would have a little under seventy seconds to justify my entire lifestyle. Then they called us to the tunnel.

As we stood there every fibre of my body came alive, with the roar of the crowd thinning to a reedy sound. We walked out and stood behind our blocks as the announcer called the finalists out and handed over control to the referee. My pulse was thumping as my brain pushed fire down my spine and into my nerves. Again, I stood motionless.

The call to the blocks was an opportunity I took quickly, instantly moving into the start position so that, with the call of 'take your marks', I could stay motion-less. I can't even remember hearing the start signal. A reflex started the dive sequence. Rapid-fire dolphin kicks pushed me to the surface and I concentrated on getting the first three strokes right. The stroke change slotted in automatically and, 6.5 seconds into the race, I was on the surface in full butterfly.

All eight swimmers hit the 25-metre mark in a row. It frightened me. I held the power output just below total maximum. I was travelling so fast that I hit the turn half a stroke earlier than I thought I would. Scrunching up my body I sped through the turn repeating the rapid dolphin kicks. Austin in Lane 3 had been beaten by the turn. Now, on the second length, I got a chance to see where Brondum was. I had half a body length on him. It wasn't over by a long chalk.

He began clawing back ground on me a centimetre at a time. Various muscle groups began to fill with lactic acid. All the time, Brondum closed the gap. I could feel my speed dropping. Almost without thinking, 'increase the power' just popped into my head. With 15 metres of the race left, every warning light on my inner dashboard went out. It was all so easy.

A series of pixels on the scoreboard said 'Giles Long GBR 1:08.24 WR'. I climbed out of the pool and could see nothing but people. Then I saw Mum and Dad jumping around. I waved frantically at them but I was completely in a trance. The marshals directed us off the pool deck, where I was interviewed first by Nick Gillingham for the BBC.

First words

Here's the transcript from the interview. I've put a † to mark the point where I snapped out of the hypnotic trance.

GL: What can I say? I've changed so much in my life. I've moved, I've changed club, I've changed this, changed that, I've moved away from my friends and tonight has all been worth it. This gold medal belongs to not only me, but my friends, my family, everyone that's ever supported me, and I just want to say, if you're listening at home, that a part of this gold medal I'm going to get is yours.

NG: Tell us all about the butterfly technique itself . . .

GL: Well it's a bit of a complicated thing in that, † er, I've worked, er, they kept changing the rules on me. And basically 'cos I was winning they thought it wasn't, they thought it was because I was make, er, taking an unfair advantage on the rules. So they kept changing the rules and making me change and, um, so I've changed . . . and I've basically stuck two fingers up to 'em. Yes, yes, yes!

NG: [laughs] I was going to say every time you keep on coming back and breaking the records. How many miles must you have swum each and every week to reach such a high level?

GL: Enough to win. Enough to win.

As I made my way through the media I gradually got sight of Colin; his eyes were full of tears. We both screamed at each other and walked down to the medallists' pen. Once I was inside he left me to go and watch the ceremony from the balcony.

As the gold medal was put around my neck I glanced down at it, unable to stop the corners of my mouth from lifting into a warm smile. 'This is what it's all about,' I thought, echoing the words Mike had said upon seeing the gold medal from the same race four years previously. The officials fell away once Emil Brondum and Ben Austin had their medals presented. I looked past twenty thousand spectators to the far end of the pool. As the Union Flag rose slowly to the sound of the national anthem, people rose to their feet.

I felt so alive but at the same time confused. The road between the two games had been rocky. I had won medals at the lowest and highest levels. I had seen my friends win and lose many times and I had watched people awarded gold medals on television many times also. Sometimes people smiled so widely you could fly a small plane between their gnashers; sometimes they cried.

I was confused because I didn't want to do any of that. I felt an inner calm, impossible to articulate. It was as if someone had taken my heart out and polished it before returning it, leaving it gleaming at the core of my soul.

I couldn't wait to share the success with my parents and jumped the security barrier into the audience. I moved quickly as I heard people say, 'Isn't that the guy who . . . ?' I eventually managed to find their seats. For about the next two minutes all we did was make silly cheering noises at one another. My aunt and uncle were there, as well as some of their friends. My uncle handed me his mobile phone with my cousin Leonie speaking from halfway across the world. I put it to my ear as she shouted '*My cousin the legend!*' It's not every day that you get to hear that.

That evening we all went to the bar of a hotel nearby. Everyone was drinking champagne, laughing and reliving bits of the race. I had a glass and tried to engage in conversation but mostly just wanted to watch everyone getting so much from something I had done. One notable absentee was my brother Magnus, who was unable to get to Sydney.

Atlanta, as it turned out, had been the warm-up. With the lack of media coverage given to the 1996 Paralympics, for most people it had finished as quickly as it had started. There had been no build-up, no getting to know the athletes. The games were on, British athletes won medals and then they were off.

In an astonishing revival of form from Atlanta, the Olympic team had produced its most impressive medal haul since the Antwerp games of 1920, jumping from thirty-sixth to tenth in the overall medals table. The UK was well and truly tuned into the inspirational Sydney games. The BBC's output of Paralympic sport also increased dramatically and with a programme on every night it made Sydney the first truly accessible games to millions. Bigwigs at the corporation were astonished by the viewing figures.

Fame

The next morning everyone was out of the house early for heats, so I took a leisurely walk up to the international zone in the village to check emails. Every 50 metres I seemed to bump into members of foreign teams congratulating me on my performance. Inside the village the conversation was always athlete to athlete. It didn't matter where you came from or your nation's politics. I headed for the Internet café and logged on. The Paralympics still had over a week to go and many were reading emails from coaches, friends and family; messages of support and luck. As soon as I put my mobile on the desk it rang. I grabbed it quickly, desperately trying not to disturb those around me, and put it to my ear. It was Joey. He had seen the race only a couple of hours previously as an edited programme on BBC television – about ten hours after it had happened. In a whisper, I said, 'Go out and have a drink for me, mate.'

'Well I was gonna talk to you about that,' he announced at the top of his voice. At that moment a whole horde of people from a bar in Old Street began singing 'Gold' by Spandau Ballet (which reached only Number 2) down the phone to me. It turned my puny Nokia mobile into a megaphone as I grinned from ear to ear trying in vain to contain the noise. People around me started smiling while pretending not to listen.

Later in the week, I was part of the 4 x 100-metre freestyle team that won gold. With James Crisp, I swam the heat and gave Marc Woods and Matt Walker a chance to rest for the final. It was one of the most thrilling races of the games with Scott Brockenshire of

Australia taking chunks out of the British lead down the home straight. Jody Cundy had enough to hang on and secure the victory.

On the final day I was set once again to swim in the heat team. This time for the 4 x 100-metre medley relay. Marc was due to swim in the morning with me giving Jody Cundy and David Roberts a chance to rest. James Crisp and Sascha Kindred swam the backstroke and breaststroke respectively (medley relay order is different from individual medley). I swam butterfly and Marc swam freestyle. The team went through third fastest into the final. Job done.

Or not. Marc and I gathered our stuff as I said to him, 'Right! It's party time, Woodsy.'

Then we stopped in our tracks as from behind us we heard, 'Just hold on a minute you two.'

Jody had been admitted to hospital with fever from an infected cut. Marc and I would be in the final after all. We got back into our swim kit and began swimming down to get rid of the lactic acid. Later, as we sat in the food hall, Marc began working out times on a piece of paper. The Canadians were going to win it, barring a disaster. But, if we could get Marc in the water within seven seconds of Australia's final swimmer, we would be in with a chance of winning the silver.

Seven seconds may sound like a vast amount of time but it's not when you consider the way that disability relays are swum. A team can have a maximum of thirty-four points, e.g. S7 + S8 + S9 + S10 = 34, which is equivalent to S7 + S7 + S10 + S10 = 34, and so on. It produces some scintillating races with the lead often changing several times as teams field athletes with different disabilities.

That evening, ours was the final race of the night and probably the most eagerly anticipated. Great Britain, the old colonial master, had robbed the Aussies of gold in the freestyle relay and the crowd were going to do everything they could to snatch one back. As we were introduced, we took a collective bow, as did the Canadians after us. Then the Australians were introduced. The exaltation of the audience was like standing under a hairdryer.

As the race got under way, James Crisp went head to head with the Aussie S9 while the Canadian S10 took the lead. After Sascha's leg we were down by about 8 metres to Australia as predicted, as they used their S10 to our S7 on the breaststroke. I would have to take a metre and a half out of Ben Austin to give us a chance of silver. I'd practised relay changeovers many times before with Marc. I knew it would be safe as soon as I hit the wall. All that was left to do was watch.

As he cut into the Australian lead the crowd hit fever pitch. We were a mere two seconds behind at the turn. They drew level with 10 metres go. The Canadians finished first and were going bananas next to us. Into the final 5 metres, and Australia were holding on. But, with 2 metres remaining, Marc scrambled for the finish, leaving the majority of twenty thousand people disappointed.

The closing ceremony put the seal on the greatest games there had ever been. With two gold medals and a silver in my bag, the journey home was the happiest long-haul flight I have ever taken.

Chapter Nine

Chinks in my Chimo

I returned to a hero's welcome. There was nothing for it but to enjoy every last moment of celebration laced with lavish attention, tinged with admiration and drenched in warmth.

Adrian Whiteson, who had been in Sydney, told me about a concert he was organising to raise money for the Teenage Cancer Trust. He was a friend of Roger Daltrey and persuaded the Who to play a charity fund raiser. In November 2000, Marc Woods and I stood in the Royal Box, with Mick Jagger in the box to our right and Jimmy Page to our left, watching the Who play their first UK gig in twenty years to a sell-out audience at the Royal Albert Hall. Halfway through the show Adrian went downstairs to make a speech on behalf of the charity. He took Marc and me with him to have a look round backstage.

We watched him walk onto the stage and begin

to speak surrounded by rock and pop legends. As he neared the end of his speech he called us both onto the stage! Absolutely terrified, I stood there as he announced us as 'both Paralympians and both gold-medallists'. I have never been so thankful for putting a medal in my pocket. I took it out and held it by the ribbon up high to the crowd. A packed Royal Albert Hall got to its feet and gave us a standing ovation. Incredible.

Having felt like a rock star for a few seconds – fulfilling a different set of teenage dreams – and with the reception invitations pouring through the letterbox it was proving difficult to get back into training. On my fridge I wanted to write, 'Say no to post-Paralympic stagnation'. But I had only enough magnetic letters for 'Don't Stob' (I'd run out of p's!). It was enough to remind me gently to ease back into the workload. I was finally starting to recognise how to switch down to small Chimo Cycles when I needed to, instead of hanging on until I was in a crisis wondering why I was even involved in the sport.

The arrival of Tony Blair as Prime Minister had signalled the country's desire for a change of direction after seventeen years of Conservative rule. He had a majority so large that he could reinstate beard tax if he had so desired. It was also the age of spin, presentation and spun presentation.

He decided to kill two birds with one stone and had the Olympic and Paralympic receptions on the same night. This meant there were far too many people to fit into Number 10, which slightly missed the point. Instead, the bash was at the Science Museum in London.

The entire place was packed and it had a certain gravitas, being surrounded by early satellites and aeroplanes. After some time, bodyguards made their way through the crowd with Tony Blair in the centre, out of reach. It couldn't have been further from John Major's intimate gathering and it was accentuated even more as he began speaking. He hardly spoke about Sydney, then switched to other matters such as the National Health Service.

Presumably, Blair's spin doctors had thought, 'Athletes are healthy people, therefore they'll be positively enthralled to hear about health.' After five minutes, a few people started booing and after ten moving away from the stage. For me, it was Cherie Blair who saved the evening as she wandered around the room chatting to people. By the time she got to me, I'd had one too many glasses of wine and for some reason I decided to paraphrase *Spinal Tap*, slurring, 'If there'sh one thing that swimming'sh taught me, it'sh to have a good time all the time.'

'Well I can certainly see you're doing that,' she retorted. As she moved on I turned back to Chris with a large smile on my face. Then she grabbed my wrist, spinning me round and said, 'Good work. Carry on.'

Paralympic plateau

As winter drew in it became harder to drag myself out of bed for training each morning. The European Championships were only eight months away, but it was looking like a bridge too far. The mood changed at Salford, almost a collective yearning to do something new. Adi decided to move to the new high-performance group that had been set up at the Manchester Aquatics Centre, which was set to be one of the key venues for the 2002 Commonwealth Games. Others stopped swimming as they found jobs. There was a sad tinge of decline to a machine that had served a purpose.

A striking, gold-embossed invitation had arrived from the Queen and Prince Philip to celebrate the achievements of the British Paralympic Team in January 2001. A few days before the event I came down with a stomach bug and heavy cold. I'd completely gone off my food and when the day itself came I was in two minds whether to go.

But I decided to grasp the opportunity. I arrived at the palace with Chris Holmes and we made our way through the iron gates and into the quadrangle that forms the central courtyard. Upon reaching the door I was shown into a separate antechamber with the other gold-medallists to meet the Queen personally before the reception got started.

The small antechamber was warm and had all of the

gold-medallists standing around three sides of the room. I stood along the back wall, opposite the door with the equestrian team standing over by the door. The room began heating up once everyone was in it and my suit started to feel pretty warm. The door to the room was closed and we were left standing for about half an hour waiting for the Queen to arrive.

Fainting fit

Eventually, the Queen was announced to the room. She made her way in with the sport minister, Kate Hoey, and began a tour of the teams. After what seemed like an age, she got to me, shook my hand and asked me about the gold medal around my neck. 'One hundred metres butterfly, ma'am.' I said. We had a brief conversation and she carried on down the line. She got to about three people past me and all of a sudden the room began to spin. I thought to myself, 'Oh, no. Not here. Not with the Queen in the room! You're not going to faint here, are you? Oh, you are.'

In a harsh whisper I said to an aide, 'I feel ill. I've got to get out of here right now.'

He said, 'Yes, sir. Come with me.'

He began leading me to the door. We got about halfway across the room and I could feel myself starting to go. As I began to stagger, Kate Hoey could see I was in trouble and began walking towards me. I thought,

'Thank God! I'm going to be saved by the minister for sport!' Instead she stuck out her hand, lifting my gold medal from off my neck. I fainted and fell out from under it with the Queen still going round the room shaking people's hands.

I woke up with Nick Webborn, the team doctor, standing over me in an adjoining ballroom. Smiling, he whispered, 'I can't wait to tell the others!'

Slowly, I gathered my thoughts and decided I had to leave. The only way out was to go back through the main reception. Ashen-faced and clutching a glass of water, I gingerly entered the room through a side door. I'd been there a few seconds when the Duke of Edinburgh wheezed, 'Well, I have to say, you look a lot better upright!' It was going from bad to worse.

Eventually I made it out of the palace and phoned my parents. I explained the whole thing to Dad and he was a true rock. 'Let's be honest, Paralympians don't have much media profile. Apart from the people there, you'll probably get away with this. Go home, put your head down; tomorrow's a new day.' It made me feel a lot better.

The next morning I woke to the sound of my mobile phone ringing. A friend on the other end said, 'Have you seen the *Daily Star*?' On Page 3, below 'Rachel' displaying her assets, they ran this headline: PARALYMPIC BRITON FAINTS IN AWE OF QUEEN.

When I got back to Salford people fell into either of two groups. A tiny minority of people were deeply worried that I was really ill. The vast majority thought it was hilarious. I think it was mentioned at every single training session for a month. The receptions and parties petered out and, as the focus switched from celebrating successes to seeking new ones, the post-games blues set in.

Crucial fulcrum

After Atlanta I'd done nothing, changed nothing, found nothing to fire the imagination and consequently the boiler of motivation was completely out of steam. I had to decide whether the love affair I had with the sport was still alive. I had to search deep within my soul as I stood at the foot of the mountain, knowing what it took to climb.

When I had first started swimming, my parents had never given me more than a nudge to get me over the crucial fulcrums of quitting. Lots of other parents had pushed their kids all the time and it had robbed them of their inner love of the sport. Even though training each day was a grind, I knew deep down inside that I still wanted to do it. On reflection, I knew that, given the chance of winning three gold medals, from three games, in one event, would be something that would drive me to the Athens Paralympics in 2004.

As Bob Dylan observed, 'The times, they are a-changin'.'

He was right but sadly wasn't on the phone giving me any more direction than that. After a lot of thought I felt I needed to get away from swimming. But how could I get away from something I needed to do every day? I took a hard look at my life and it was all swimming, morning, noon and night. Most of my friends from university had gravitated towards London and so, provided I could join a good club, that was what I would do. This was the start of a new Chimo Cycle and perhaps the first one I had ever fully envisaged before embarking upon it.

It was late spring when Chris Holmes first put me in touch with Rhys Gormley at Barnet Copthall in north London. Although Chris had produced disappointing results in Sydney, he had done some great swimming at the club, and Rhys was constantly proving his record with rising star Sarah Price, who was tearing up the able-bodied backstroke world rankings. I went for a trial with Rhys's group and was invited to join.

The decision illuminated my future as if a switch had been flicked on. It transferred into results within days and ultimately into qualification for the European Championships. At Barnet, training was based on target times. They always had to be bettered and done with greater ease. The very foundation of every training session was change.

In Stockholm I discovered that Emil Brondum had retired; and, although he posted a fast heat time, Kostas

Fykas let his emotions get the better of him in the call-up room before the final. He swam slightly more slowly, handing me the race. I was half a second off my best but it would be good to move to Barnet with recent success under my belt.

Back in the UK, I started sorting out the move to London. Joey was coming to the end of his rental agreement and we had agreed to look for a place together.

At Salford we started morning training at a civilised seven o'clock. At Copthall it was back to the gruelling 5.30 a.m. starts. There was no messing about with Rhys, too. If you weren't in the building by 5.20 a.m. he locked the door; everyone was in the water on the stroke of half past.

The review of Lottery funding took place every year in January and could be a very nerve-racking time indeed. With a highly successful British team and a limited pot of money, consideration times were tight across the three funding bands. To secure A-funding, a swimmer had to hit a time that was inside the world record plus 1 per cent. But I held the world record and consequently had nothing to worry about.

In 2002, Manchester was to be the host city for the Commonwealth Games. In 1998 the games had taken a retrograde step when the Malaysian organisers had excluded disability events. In Manchester, they would once again be included but in a strange format called multi-disability. Full inclusion was not an option but, rather than pick a couple of class-specific events, they would create a new system allowing swimmers of differing disabilities to compete against each other. As in Victoria eight years earlier, there would be only the 50- and 100-metre freestyle, though the winner wouldn't necessarily be the person who touched the wall first. Instead, it would be the swimmer who was the closest to the world record in their class. In essence, it made a sport that was already complicated almost impenetrable.

I was desperate to compete and said some fairly harsh words in print, which I wished I'd not. One of the milder quotes in the *Telegraph* read, 'It's going to be like putting a super-tanker and a rowing boat in the water next to each other.' Even though I was without a chance of qualifying, I still went to the trials to compete. Rhys had the entire squad fully tapered and rested. Thirty-six hours before the event started, I really began to motor. Sarah Price was already the short-course world record holder of the 200-metre backstroke and qualified with ease. Her rolling style of backstroke looked as effortless as the gliding shoulder blades of a tiger in the long grass.

I decided that I had no chance of qualifying for the games, and so decided to swim butterfly in the 100-metre freestyle, an event with no rules governing stroke style. I felt amazing in the heat and felt sure I could dip under the world record in the final. I just missed it, clocking 1:08.31. More importantly than that, it proved to me that Rhys's system worked.

World Championships

Every Monday Rhys held a team meeting. Most of the time they were very short, lasting not much more than five minutes. Sometimes they could last for a lot longer if he felt the time was better spent discussing the way forward than churning out metres in the pool. Every week something was changed. At times there was a huge shift of emphasis in the programme's composition; at others a tiny tweak of approach to one aspect or another. There was always something new to conquer, even in the pitch-black January mornings with not a major competition in sight.

Later that spring I qualified for the World Championships in Mar del Plata, Argentina. It would be the first time the world's best swimmers had come together for over two years. China had won the right to stage the Olympic and Paralympic Games. A country of over a billion people that officially had no disabled citizens suddenly acquired 60 million overnight, with the overall total thought to be more in the region of 200 million. Clouds were gathering for a storm from the East.

I couldn't hide my disappointment at not competing in the lavishly staged Commonwealth Games. I had wanted to compete on home soil in a major competition since childhood. So, when the chance came to go to France with some friends while it was on, I didn't think twice. Nonetheless, I monitored results from across the Channel. It was great to see my club teammate, Sarah Price, win both the 100- and 200-metre backstroke. As I stood in a *boulangerie* – a bakery – on 3 August 2002, I got a text message saying that Adi had won a silver in the 200-metre individual medley, having won bronze in the 400-metre IM the day before.

One swimmer with a disability who had truly shone was Natalie du Toit of South Africa. But on the whole it saddened me to hear the way the multi-disability system had been received. It had been inevitable that people wouldn't understand the way it was structured and I couldn't help but feel that a lot of work that had gone into generating credibility had been undone.

The journey to Mar del Plata was arduous: a long-haul flight to Buenos Aires, then a five-hour bus ride south to the holiday resort that had hosted the Pan American Games in 1995. Argentina was in the grip of a deep recession, but upon our arrival it was obvious that these people lived life to the full. As the wind rolled in off the southern Atlantic Ocean, paragliders dangled a few feet above the traffic, weaving their way in and out of power lines.

Having checked into the hotel, we made our way down to a substandard pool. In a one-hour training session the water turned the white on Union Flag swimming hats to brown, and the decking around the floor was so rotten that one wrong move could put you out of the competition. Some of the more explosive starters actually began tearing the tops off the blocks. Anne Green was still ruling the roost and could be seen at every session wandering round with the organisers, bellowing orders while jabbing a pointed finger at everything that was wrong.

Four days before the competition started, I felt heavy. My stroke felt as if it had no panache. With two days to go, I began to get worried, as my physiology remained entrenched. I couldn't get through to Rhys on the phone and it was all I could do to keep my nerves under control.

As the competition started, I knew I wasn't at my best. Sometimes, you can do absolutely everything right that's inside your control and it still just doesn't happen. The start sheet showed an anomaly in the form of Xiao Fu Wang, entered for the S8 100-metre butterfly. His time said 1:10.00. It was clearly made up but the question remained: was he faster or slower than his entry time?

Due to lack of money, lots of countries would compete internationally only at the World Championships or the Paralympics, which made it difficult to keep track of their times. China uses this to its advantage and never publishes the times of its athletes. When he came within a whisker of breaking my world record in the heats, I had my answer.

For me the first race felt laboured. With my brother travelling in Argentina, my parents had decided that they would fly out too. Security at the event was so lax that spectators mingled with the teams on the poolside. Dad came down to the diving pool with me after the race and we experimented with a few changes. But it was clear that I just wasn't going to turn myself into sparkling form in the space of half an hour.

In the late-afternoon sun in early December, I lost the 100-metre butterfly and, not for the first time, slipped off the top of the world ranking list. Wang had smashed my record into smithereens, a time of 1:06.84 glaring back at me from the board. My time of 1:08.79 was some way off my best. It left me with an empty echoing feeling inside. In New Zealand I'd thrown it away; this time it was taken from me and I immediately wanted it back. I wandered back to the rest of the team and simply said, 'Bollocks!'

My butterfly time had not been good enough for me to stand a chance of swimming as part of the medley relay. I gave myself some stern words that evening preparing to throw absolutely everything I had at the 200-metre IM the next day. That evening, Glen went to work on my shoulder. He said, 'Mate, I was really impressed by the way you handled that disappointment today. Other people have spat the dummy out in the last couple of days after similar things.' Those few basic words made a world of difference. It was the first time I really became aware of the way in which people in a fully functioning team fulfil many more roles than those written down on paper.

On Day 3 of the meet I still felt weighed down.

Still, I attacked the heats and posted a time just two-tenths away from my best. I went back to the hotel and rested.

In the final I pushed it to the absolute limit. My lungs were screaming. I didn't listen, just pushed. I looked round and saw 2:39.46. I had managed to lower my personal best (or managed 'to PB', as we say) by just over half a second and amazingly won the bronze medal by a few hundredths. I hauled myself out of the pool and immediately reached for my inhaler. My lungs began to ease as I was marshalled into the medallists' pen.

The pool was hot as the intense sunlight poured through the roof and danced on the unclean water. As I awaited the walk to the podium I wondered what I could change.

Chapter Ten

In Pursuit of Time

I didn't even want to show anyone the silver and bronze that I had won. So I put them in the shoebox where I kept all of my 'stepping-stone' medals. Finding one and a half seconds wouldn't be easy, but inside I genuinely believed it was possible.

I contemplated taking performance-enhancing drugs to bridge the chasm. Could I achieve the necessary times without intervention? But that Christmas, when I was at my parents' house, they were talking about how proud they were of everything I'd achieved in the pool. There are times when you realise how many people it takes to put you where you want to be. This was one of those times. How could I have ever even contemplated risking their pride?

Of course, I could clearly remember how one blood transfusion made me buzz with energy. That must be the sensation that dope cheats enjoy. However, if you take performance-enhancing drugs it has one of three outcomes: (1) you get away with it; (2) you get caught; or (3) it kills you. The one thing they all have in common is that, deep down inside, *you* know that you are a cheat until the day you die.

When I stood on the rostrum receiving my gold medal after my 100-metre butterfly swim in Sydney, I knew that I had produced the best performance of my life. It felt pure. The very distillation of inner calm collected in a flask and sealed for ever. Had I taken drugs to help me do it, I would have felt polluted.

I truly believe I have never raced against anyone on drugs. There is still little money in Paralympic sport. Taking drugs and getting away with it (which, let's face it, is the important bit) is incredibly expensive. But Paralympic athletes are just as desperate to win as their able-bodied counterparts; consequently, cheating has happened.

At the Sydney Paralympic games eleven people were stripped of medals after positive dope tests. Then there was high-profile cheating of an entirely different nature. The Spanish Paralympic basketball team won gold at Sydney. Then it was revealed than ten out of twelve squad members were not, in fact, competing with an intellectual disability. Their claims of having an IQ of less than seventy were false. Now a different competition is held for sportspeople with intellectual disability.

There's the dubious practice of boosting, in which

genuinely disabled people enhance their fight-or-flight responses by sitting on tacks, for example, or turning off catheters. Their bodies cannot feel the discomfort because of their disability but the brain issues a huge boost of adrenalin, giving their performance extra edge.

Some disabled competitors are less than honest about their condition. Often, these individuals seem to lack the excited spark of others. Just because spectators don't know that someone's cheating, it doesn't mean their teammates won't. For some, the desire to exploit the system is paramount.

When I hear of athletes using drugs to go faster, reach higher, be stronger or indulge in other dubious practices, I just feel sad. No one truly gets away with it because you can never escape yourself.

So it was a Chimo-style approach that I opted for rather than that of manmade chemical compounds. Rhys and I drew up a list of potential improvements, changes that hadn't worked as we'd anticipated and some completely new ways of training.

Tim Reddish, a former Paralympic swimmer, became performance director. Within weeks, Tim installed Lars Humer as GB head coach.

Swedish swimmer Therese Alshammar began training at Copthall. She was a double-Olympic silver-medallist from Sydney and had won eight World Championship gold medals across two competitions. Built for speed, she was living proof that metres in the pool do not always equal medals. When she handed Rhys her training logs, he said that there had not been a week in the previous four years when she had swum more than 20 kilometres. There were eleven-year-olds at Copthall who swam further.

Different strokes for different folks

Every athlete has a specific physiological composition. In broad terms, there are two types of muscle fibre: fast-twitch and slow-twitch. Sprinters have a higher proportion of fast-twitch fibres; they are born with them. An individual can train their fast-twitch fibres to work at an optimal level but they cannot increase the number they have. Large-volume training just didn't work for Therese, so specialised was her physiology. So Rhys began a sprint lane, though he was convinced that if she increased her weekly distance she would improve.

From my own perspective, it was great to have another person on the squad who was my age. Since Chris had retired, it had been just Sarah Price and me. Most swimmers get to around eighteen years old and, if they are good enough to make it internationally, they continue; if not, they finish. Thus, the average age of the squad remained the same as I got older.

The ventilation in the training pool at Barnet Copthall was particularly poor and I had been stopped from using my inhaler because I couldn't medically prove that I needed it. On a simple peak-flow test my lung function appeared to be very good. But I knew something was wrong every time I began coughing heavily when working hard. Sometimes, if it was really bad, it would affect other people too, but I always seemed to start first. It wasn't a new problem but one that I had learned to manage. I tried to get my inhaler back, but, without proof that I needed it, I would test positive in a doping-control test.

I carried on busting a gut in training but just didn't seem to be getting the rewards in races. My weekly output on a tough week could be as high as 50,000 metres, a long way on one arm. Dad would watch me train and pick up on minor technical faults. I spent a lot of time working on core stability and a wide range of land training techniques. With just my left arm at full extension above my head, I had no trouble in throwing a 3-kilo medicine ball repeatedly at a wall.

In 2003 a financial crisis had arisen in the European Paralympic Committee. Somewhere along the line someone had made the ridiculous decision that the European Championships should be opened up to countries outside of the Continent. This practically tripled the cost of the competition and nowhere could afford to stage it. It was hard to maintain focus with such a long time between major competitions and it also had other knock-on effects. In March I had moved into a flat with Lynne, my then girlfriend. I was slightly uneasy about how she would react in the final few months before the games. The Europeans would provide a good taster. Without them it would be straight into the Paralympics.

Rhys began giving me more sessions in the sprint lane. I still wasn't getting the rewards in races. But I kept changing tiny aspects of my strokes, as if searching for the edges of a door in the dark, trying to figure out a way of levering it open just enough to move through it and on to the next level. At times my lack of progress was so slow that it came close to crushing my motivation altogether. On those days I would concentrate on a single stroke at a time, often varying my hand pitch by mere millimetres.

In the summer I swam well at nationals but I still hadn't managed to crack the 68-second mark for the 100-metre butterfly. It was becoming a standing joke. Barnet wasn't working for Therese. She spent a lot of time travelling around Europe competing for cash prizes. When she had an opportunity to move back to Stockholm, she took it.

In September, the team went to Cyprus for a training camp. We arrived in Nicosia and, as always, headed straight to the pool. Working with Lars Humer was always productive. He approached swimming with the same mindset as I did: always looking for the alteration that would give that little bit extra. He understood the motivating power of change and came up with 'the orb of technique'. It was just a bouncy ball but it was awarded to the swimmer in his lane who had made the most significant positive technical change in the session. It started off as a joke but by the end of week one it was fiercely contested. With a simple tool he had created individual Chimo Cycles for everyone in the lane as well as having them working as a unit.

I had a list of things in my mind that I wanted to achieve, primarily changes to my butterfly that were not textbook adjustments but that I felt might make me quicker. In the two weeks off, I had tried to gather all of my past experience from the development of one-armed butterfly, and breathing to the right while stroking to the left. I refined it down to three areas that I would concentrate on.

First, I tried to keep as much of my body out of the water as possible. As I lifted my head higher, my hips would fall, so I would try to lift them back to where they had been. When my left arm was out of the water, my right shoulder wanted to dip, so I worked on stabilising it. I was trying to lift my body out of the water using only the water to press on; it was a perpetual balancing act.

Second, I tried to remain as flat on the water as possible. If the advantage of breathing to the side is that you get to travel in a straighter line, make sure you use it. It sounds simple, but it had new effects on the rate at which I had to turn my head, when I turned it and how far I turned it. Because my mouth was so much closer to the water, I had to turn my head almost past 90 degrees. Drawing air in rapidly through a twisted windpipe could be quite hard work.

Finally, I improved the connection between the power sources. I wanted to make sure that the dolphin kicks were in exact synchronisation with my hand entering and exiting the water.

Every single stroke of butterfly, on every single length of every single session, I tried to do these three things. About ten days into the three-week camp, something clicked and I just seemed to move forward without any effort at all, as if I had found the door. The difference was so profound that I told Lars about it straightaway. This new way of swimming periodically slipped away and returned several times at first until I managed to embed it as habit.

Rhys put me in the sprint lane full-time on my return and I just seemed to cut up and down the 25-metre pool as if it were just 10 metres. Because I was travelling with a much higher efficiency, I needed to breathe less, which in turn meant I could maintain a more streamlined position for a greater proportion of the race.

Personal best

At the National Short Course Championships in Sheffield that November, the results were mind-blowing. None of my best results had ever been set in races scheduled in the morning. On the Saturday, I was in the 100-metre freestyle, one of the very first events. In the race I felt like the ball of a pinball machine bouncing up and down the pool. With disbelief I read 1:03.71 next to my name. It is simply unheard of for a senior athlete to drop over two seconds over a 100-metre race. But the best was still to come. In the 100-metre butterfly I felt as if I could have cut glass. There was so much time for everything to fit within the stroke. It felt so good that, if I could have stepped out of my body to let someone else have a go, I would. The time: 1:05.46. We were back in business, thanks to the Chimo tactics that I had instinctively adopted. Now all I needed to do was convert it to a long-course time in preparation for the Paralympic Trials in March.

That autumn, Sarah Price said she wanted to talk to me. Something was clearly eating away at her and we agreed to meet up for lunch a few days later. Before we made it to the café, she had decided to leave the club. Rhys and Sarah had always had a boom/bust relationship. That November was bust. They finally parted company after a successful time together. I had seen swimmers switch coaches and clubs close to big competitions before, but never seen anyone pull it off. In every club change I had ever made it had taken me a year to settle. There were frenzied efforts to repair the relationship from all areas of British swimming. Unfortunately, the die had been cast.

I hadn't seen Adi for ages, though we kept in touch.

He had subsequently moved to Stockport Metro and had been improving steadily. Once again, the Olympics were on his radar. I thought there was a fault with the phone when he told me that he'd broken his collarbone, three months before the Olympic Trials.

He'd been messing about with his housemate in the kitchen. Now, if you decide to get involved with a man whose nickname is the Barbarian you're probably not going to come out of it all that well. Steve Parry had sent Adi headlong into a kitchen cupboard with unintentional force. Once again, Adi's dreams of going to the games hung in the balance.

Rule reorganisation

At Copthall I continued to work in the sprint lane and the technical form carried on into the New Year. To qualify for the Athens Paralympics, trials were split into two stages. Although the qualifying standard had to be hit at only one, both competitions were required by the selectors to be of exceptional standard. Not long before the first stage at a competition in Manchester, I heard that Ben Austin had posted a time of one minute and six seconds on the *Swimming Australia* website. How on Earth had he managed to drop three seconds overnight? He was one of the best S8 100-metre freestyle swimmers in the world but his style of one-arm swimming was completely different from mine. With the focus all on power, he had never been able to master breathing to the opposite side.

After a bit of investigation, I found out that the rule that had been put in place ten years earlier at the World Championships in Malta had been revoked. I bumped into Anne Green, head of swimming with the International Paralympic Committee, at a competition in France and took the opportunity to find out what had happened.

Trying desperately to not sound accusatory, I asked her about the rule change and if it meant that I could go back to breathing to the same side as my stroking arm. She kept um-ing and ah-ing and must have seen that I was desperate for an answer. 'Well, technically, yes,' she said. In this context I wasn't sure what other kind of yes there was. When she said that the rule change had been in effect since the middle of 2003, my jaw was on the floor. It became clear that even after the rule change in 1994 no one-armed swimmer was managing to keep their shoulders entirely level. I have never managed to decide entirely whether that meant, 'We've made it too difficult so we're switching it back.'

A small part of me felt pretty smug for finally being proved right, but mostly alarm bells started ringing. This opened up the butterfly event to a group of excep-tional freestyle swimmers.

I have a lot of respect for Anne. She has driven Paralympic swimming forward, continued to build its credibility and taken many decisions that have made her unpopular, decisions that many would have shied from. But all the respect in the world didn't change the fact that I had to revert to a style of butterfly that I hadn't used competitively for almost ten years, and have it mastered in six months. My swimming career had been completely turned on its head. Having spent seasons looking for change, I now had it heaped upon me.

In April, the form that I had at the Short Course Nationals carried over as I clocked 1:05.81 in the 100-metre freestyle and 1:07.03 in the 100-metre butterfly at the first stage of Paralympic Trials in Sheffield. I swam both exactly the same, except for the turn, which in butterfly demands that the competitor touch the wall with the hands first. In freestyle, a tumble-turn is the quickest route to planting the feet on the wall. The turn had not been a good one in the butterfly, and, in analysis after the race, Rhys, Dad and I decided it probably added an extra half a second. It had surprised me how easy it was to revert to racing the way I had so many years earlier, but also that it hadn't produced a much faster time. Since 1994, I had altered and refined my opposite-side breathing stroke so many times that I could now adjust any part of the stroke I wanted to. But it simply wasn't giving me enough time.

Walking down the poolside, Rhys and I decided that we had to take a gamble. If we carried on doing what we were doing, my results would probably stay the same. Rhys had an idea of where we might be able to find some more time. He wanted to increase the number and intensity of sets that I swam at top speed in training. I agreed and we shook hands on it.

I moved over to where the Stockport Metro Swimming Club was standing on poolside. They already had three Olympic qualifiers: James Goddard, Graeme Smith and Steve Parry. Now it was Adi's turn in the 200-metre IM. With the wire still connecting the two halves of his collarbone together, he stood behind the blocks. The injury had given him a new intensity of focus in the final few weeks leading into the trials, and he was going to need to be as sharp as possible if he was to qualify. It would take nothing less than his life-time best to make it to the games. No one on the poolside was more nervous than Steve.

Even at the very start of the race it was clear that it going to be between Adi and Robin Francis to his left. His butterfly looked good and both men went around the first turn together. Adi lost ground on backstroke but clawed it all back on breaststroke. He was still slightly behind as they both switched to the final freestyle length. With 25 metres to go, both of them were clearly throwing absolutely every last drop of energy into the race. With 15 to go Adi drew level. They both thundered into the final 10, then 5, 4, 3, 2 . . . There was an almighty spray of water as both hit the wall simultaneously. All eyes switched up to the board. Adi had been beaten by a few hundredths of a second, but it didn't matter, because both had gone under the qualifying time. Sarah Price also qualified in the 200-metre backstroke but, on that day, no one wanted to go to the games more than Adrian Turner.

Divergence

The Olympic and Paralympic Trials are not a particularly pleasant competition, principally because the vast majority of people leave disappointed. The euphoria of qualification quickly slides away, revealing the task ahead. From that point on, the two teams diverge in their preparation.

Within days we were back on the plane to Cyprus for training. I got to work on the plan agreed with Rhys. I began practising the self-hypnosis that I used before each major competition.

Upon return it wasn't long before we were at second-stage qualification. Having already qualified, I decided not to taper for the competition; as expected, my times were not as quick as they had been earlier in the year. With this competition out of the way, all that separated me from the games was a long summer stretching out before me.

Also, I had the additional help of being able to use my inhaler again. A test had finally been designed to separate those who *needed* to use one from those who *wanted* to use one. Frustration was finally ended when I was diagnosed with mild exercise-induced asthma.

As the weather got hotter I began to focus to a higher intensity and became characteristically icy as I began slowly to wind up mentally towards the race. It was a hard time for Lynne, sharing a flat with someone who became more emotionally detached by the day.

Before the team flew out to Cyprus we had the opportunity of watching friends and teammates competing at the Olympics in Athens on television. With a few exceptions it wasn't going well. Many complained of feeling tired and heavy; something had clearly gone wrong in their preparation. One absolute joy was to see Steve Parry winning a bronze medal in the 200-metre butterfly. He had been fourth more times than I could remember at major international meets. The beaming smile on his face was magical; he even did a little dance when he got out of the pool.

Watching the Olympics always gave a boost to the Paralympians waiting in the wings. Rhys and I didn't speak much as we flew out to Nicosia. We were concentrating on the job in hand. He would be with me for the all-important holding camp before flying back home when the team moved on to Athens. We got stuck into the precision process of the taper.

With every major competition I have ever been to, the final few days made the competition feel further away than it did six months previous. It is perhaps because life is stripped to the bear essentials for swimming, so you can become plain bored.

When the holding camp was complete, Rhys wished me the very best of luck. With that, we packed our things and went our separate ways. It was as if another onion skin of team protection had been stripped away, leaving me just that little bit more exposed. It would keep happening until I was standing behind the block on my own.

Athens

When we arrived in Athens it was a completely new experience. In Atlanta, the organisers didn't really want us there; the audience took a while to warm up but ended up loving it. In Sydney, the whole place was rocking from beginning to end. In Athens, most of the city residents went on holiday because it was going to be too crowded during the Olympics. I guess you can't please all the people all the time.

However, as the final days approached before the opening ceremony, a buzz picked up around the city, and inside the athletes' village it was electric. People with steely faces moved around food halls, transport malls and apartment blocks. The atmosphere was charged with the idea that somewhere in Athens was a room containing a stack of medals. The only question was who was going to win them.

A day before the opening ceremony, I glimpsed the different ways in which people regard their disabilities. A long table in the dining hall was completely filled with British team members. Half were swimmers and the other half were powerlifters. I was sitting halfway along, opposite a fairly mean-looking powerlifting coach.

People were speculating about what would happen at the opening ceremony and how it would differ from the Olympics. Sascha Kindred, who sat at the far end, said he had seen a giant tree outside the stadium. James Crisp had heard something surreal about people from each disability group being carried towards the tree on trays from the four corners of the stadium. Now the ideas were really starting to flow. Then someone shouted out, 'They've all got hooks on their shirts and are going to be hung on the branches making a disability Christmas tree!' The entire swimming team was roaring with laughter – and on it went. 'No, it's a healing tree! After tomorrow night we'll all be fixed. There'll be no disabled people left and it'll double up as the closing ceremony, too!' We had tears rolling down our faces. I looked at the powerlifting coach sitting opposite. With a stony face she got up and walked away.

Although curious to see what they were going to do with the huge tree, I decided not to go to the opening, although the buzz in the flat when those who had gone returned was exhilarating.

When race day finally came I was good to go. That

morning I shaved and quietly looked myself in the eye before walking to the food hall for solitary breakfast. When I arrived early at the pool, there was no activity bar the American team, who had had to use special buses with armed bodyguards on, so weren't so flexible in the times they could choose. But quiet was good.

Warm-up felt sharp. I was ready to race and prepared. I was on the start sheet in Lane 4 of Heat 1. Both Austin and Wang were in Heat 2. As I made my way through the marshalling stages, I could feel my heart beginning to strike hammer blows. In the call-up room I said nothing except to confirm my name to the steward. The arena was packed. There wasn't even standing room. As I took my tracksuit off I thought, 'You can do this.' As I had many times before, I licked the inside of my goggles to stop them from misting and waited for the call to the blocks.

A long blast of the referee's whistle initiated the start sequence. To the sound of the gun we were off. Work in the gym paid off, as my powerful start launched me forward. It was as if I were racing in a time warp, swimming the way I had at my first international in 1993. I was at the 50-metre halfway mark before I knew it and heading back. I decided to push the race hard but not to the point of destruction, and when I finished the clock read '1:07.34, Paralympic Record'. The crowd went wild. Knowing what was coming next, I remained circumspect.

Both Wang and Austin went under the new mark. It was Austin who set the record; he'd gone absolutely flat out to make a point. But Wang was doing just enough to make it through to the next round and secure a good lane. The gold was out of reach for me but the fight for the silver was still alive. I got changed and headed back to the village. I lay on my bed and concentrated on making sure I was mentally cool but excited.

When the final came that evening, I was in Lane 3, Austin in Lane 4 and Wang in Lane 5. It was a configuration that would form a spectacular overhead photo that made up the centrefold of *Observer Sport Monthly*. Kostas Fykas drew the largest cheer from the Greek audience but I knew it would be between the three of us.

Racing uncertainty

In the silence just before the start I could hear my pulse. At 25 metres we were all in a line. I looked out at both of them. As we reached the end of the first length both of them had just moved in front of me. I pulled it all back coming out of the turn. I pushed myself relentlessly in the final 20 metres. I put in an additional spurt in the final 10 but I didn't even have to look at the board to know where I had finished.

The bronze medal lay round my neck and I watched

the Union Flag slowly rise to the sound of the Chinese National Anthem. Inside I felt an array of emotions that I had never felt before. Looking back, I realise it was perhaps the first time in swimming that I finally felt as if I'd reached the destination, after continually travelling for so long. Being a sporting competitor is always more about the journey than the destination. But had I forgotten to pull over and have a brief look round on the way? Had the fuel of massive, middling and incremental change been too potent ever to allow the vehicle of inspiration and motivation to pause long enough for me to absorb the surroundings fully?

I had paused once, had a big look round and ground to a complete halt. That occasion, after Atlanta 1996, had nearly cost me my entire career. Because I had no change to give me new ideas, there was no inspiration; and how can anyone be motivated without that? Without motivation I was never going to do anything; consequently, nothing changed.

The cycle of change, producing *in*spiration, producing *mo*tivation, producing change and so on is one that can be kick-started by an initial spark generated from within or from someone close by. I have been fortunate to experience Paralympics at the end of some of my largest Chimo Cycles. Some of those cycles were started by me and some from the inspiration provided by others.

It was good luck that I was in the right place at the right time when those cycles were started by other people. It's a cliché, but I do believe you make your own luck. Perhaps wanting to be inspired in the first place was the making of that luck. But, even if you are going to keep an open mind and hope that someone comes along and says something profound and eloquent, you might be waiting a long time. So why not change something now and kick-start your Chimo Cycle right away?

Chapter Eleven

Bowing Out

In the New Year Honours of 2006 I was awarded the MBE. As I walked towards the Queen standing on a red-carpeted dais, hoping that she didn't recognise me as the fainting man of yesteryear, my left eyelid got the jitters. A lack of sleep over the festive season had taken its toll and left me feeling that I was winking at her. She pinned the medal to my chest and, as I turned to walk back, I felt awash with pride. All the medals I had won in swimming had always felt primarily mine. I never forgot the numerous people who had helped me to get there, but nonetheless I had been the one fighting tooth and nail in the race.

This time it was different. The MBE feels as if it belongs to those around me, as if in some way it is their recognition for sticking by me.

Nearly six months earlier, on 6 July 2005, I was in Trafalgar Square when London was awarded the right to host the Olympics and Paralympics in 2012. Before the announcement the atmosphere was thick with anxiety, the buildings around the square almost groaning in anticipation. Whirring round in my head I kept hearing the flippant summary I'd given lots of people about our chances of winning. 'We've got the best bid but Paris has got the most stuff built. It's a question of if they believe we can do what we say we can.'

Not an entirely erudite way of estimating our chances but nevertheless fairly succinct. It was evidently fairly persuasive: I received emails from a few people thanking me because they'd put a bet on the outcome.

When the word 'London' exited the International Olympic Committee's president Jacque Rogge's mouth in Singapore, everything and everyone exploded. I instantly knew that I wanted to be there in 2012. I wanted to compete. When I had first decided I wanted to compete at the Olympics it was a dream. The way things turned out I took a slightly different path, a parallel path where, among the dark still shards of shattered dreams, the seeds of change found fertile ground. Constant innovation helped me to achieve my dream, and surely it could again.

Effects of age

To compete in the games on home soil was a long-held ambition. But I had to concede that this was now surely a dream too far. To compete at an Olympics or Paralympics is a once-in-a-lifetime opportunity. To compete in such a prestigious contest on home ground is rarer still.

Sadly, there isn't a motivational tool in the world that is sufficiently powerful to combat the effects of age. By the time I finished swimming I was still improving, though each personal best became more elusive. Every sport must move faster than any one individual. Without its constant hunger to consume and reinvent itself it would be pointless. In March 2007 I retired from competitive swimming.

It was a massive change. I was thirty-one and had been a member of a swimming club for over twenty-three years. The day I retired was the only time I have ever talked about past achievements at a training session and then left the pool with dry hair.

But I had seen this before and I knew that this was precisely the period that I had to keep on driving change in order to move forward. I had spent a lot of time talking to kids in schools after the Athens games. I have been lucky enough to meet some inspirational people and the value of inspiring people is something you cannot put a price on.

In January 2006 I became a motivational and inspirational speaker for business organisations. I love the adrenalin rush from public speaking that almost emulates that of racing. Talking to people afterwards and leaving them energised creates a tremendous feeling and with each speech there is the possibility that I have sparked someone else's Chimo Cycle.

However, the speaking part of being a professional speaker is only the fun part. There are still all of the other pieces of running a business successfully that are far less exciting. I have target ideas of where I would like the business to be in three years' time, but the link between that goal and updating the website is probably not enough to make me really get stuck into it. Instead, I create a Chimo Cycle over a much shorter period of time. The harder I find it to sit down and do the task, the smaller the initial change. But, once that first small cycle has started, I can use it to spark another one, until I have a set of small cycles that are supporting a larger one that encompasses bigger change, which needs more inspiration for even more motivation. I think of the tiny Chimo Cycles as ball bearings that support the whole vehicle.

As I said at the beginning of the book, the Chimo Cycle wasn't something I was aware of when I was swimming. But when I look back at my career it's what I did. When I was at my most successful I used the processes of *ch*ange, *i*nspiration, *mo*tivation – Chimo – on a length-by-length, session-by-session, daily, weekly, monthly, yearly basis. When at my least successful, I barely used it at all. After twenty years I know it works and I still use it today.

I hope it works for you, too.

Index